INVITATION TO
CROSS-CULTURAL
THEOLOGY

Also by William A. Dyrness

Learning About Theology from the Third World

INVITATION TO CROSS-CULTURAL THEOLOGY

Case Studies
In Vernacular
Theologies

WILLIAM A. DYRNESS

ZondervanPublishingHouse
Academic and Professional Books
Grand Rapids, Michigan

A Division of HarperCollins*Publishers*

Invitation to Cross-Cultural Theology
Copyright © 1992 by William A. Dyrness

Requests for information should be addressed to:
Zondervan Publishing House
Academic and Professional Books
Grand Rapids, Michigan 49530

Library of Congress Cataloging-in-Publication Data

Dyrness, William A.
    Invitation to cross-cultural theology : case studies in vernacular
theologies / William A. Dyrness.
        p.   cm.
    Includes bibliographical references and index.
    ISBN 0-310-53581-6
    1. Theology–Methodology–Case studies. 2. Christianity and
culture–Case studies. I. Title.
BR118.D97 1992
230'.09–dc20   92-11646
                                                                      CIP

Permission for "Protestant Maya Text" (abridged), written by David
Scotchmer, is granted by the Institute for Mesoamerican Studies, The
University at Albany, State University of New York. It first appeared in
Symbol and Meaning Beyond the Closed Community, Gary H. Gossen,
editor.

Permission for "Traveling Preacher in North China" is granted by the William
Carey Library, Pasadena, California. It is published as Interview 5.13 in *Wise
as Serpents, Harmless as Doves*, by Jonathan Chao and Richard van Houten,
1988, pp. 201–11.

All Scripture quotations, unless otherwise noted and excluding the
appendices, are taken from the HOLY BIBLE: NEW INTERNATIONAL
VERSION (North American Edition). Copyright © 1973, 1978, 1984, by the
International Bible Society. Used by permission of Zondervan Bible
Publishers.

Edited by Jan M. Ortiz
Cover design by The Aslan Group

Printed in the United States of America

91 92 93 94 95 96 /   / 10 9 8 7 6 5 4 3 2 1

CONTENTS

To
Grace Williams Dyrness
My mother, who taught me much of what I know
about the theology of everyday life

PREFACE

This book seeks to give serious theological attention to the way ordinary Christians, in a variety of settings, think about and live out their Christian faith. Several recent influences have been important in laying the groundwork for such a project. On the one hand, anyone who has tried to capture the emphases of theology done outside a Western academic setting becomes aware of how limited a perspective one gains from listening only to the written sources. While these obviously cannot be ignored, there are worlds of experience and of faith that lie outside bound covers. Robert Schreiter has done much to call our attention to these alternative sources and to suggest how best to learn from them. He notes: "To develop local theologies. . .one must listen to popular religion in order to find out what is moving in people's lives. Only then can local theologies be developed and the liberating power of the gospel come to its full flower" (1985:143).

On the other hand, some important work of sociologists who are sensitive to the religious and theological dimension of life has made interesting use of narrative in getting at a people's values. Robert Bellah and his colleagues used people's stories to discover some basic American attitudes toward individualism and community in their best-selling book *Habits of the Heart* (1985). More recently Robert Wuthnow, in *Acts of Compassion* (1991), has used a similar technique to describe contemporary attitudes toward caring in America. In this book Wuthnow says of people who are involved regularly in volunteer work: "Their stories scarcely gave a full or logical account of their motives. But they did provide an explanation of how and why these people had become involved in caring. Having stories to tell was a vitally important part of their caring" (1991:85). It strikes me that this is, if anything, more true for people who follow Christ. From the beginning, the stories of faith have been central to the growth of the church and, I would argue, to the handing down of the Christian tradition.

So, a concern to listen to voices otherwise excluded from the theological conversation along with tools provided by the social sciences have made it possible for theologians to think about what my colleague Robert Banks calls a "theology of everyday life" (1987). As will soon become clear, what exactly this should look like and how it will survive the rough handling that academics ordinarily give this kind of thing is not at all clear. But after some experience hearing and collecting these accounts of faith, it is hard to deny the theological significance either of the materials themselves or of the work of recording and reflecting on them.

We acknowledge that this small study represents only the very first steps toward thinking systematically and critically about the way various Christian communities express their faith. In order to do this we have collected stories that recount people's experience with God from five very different communities around the world. These are obviously meant to be representative examples of communities with deep and long-standing experiences of believing and following Christ. Other peoples in other places might just as easily have been chosen, but these represent the particular network of experience and relationships of this author.

Obviously a study of this kind would not be possible apart from the generous cooperation of many people who have provided links with these communities—to say nothing of the willingness of the people themselves. Most significant has been Professor David Scotchmer of Dubuque Theological Seminary, whose long work with the Mam Indians in Guatemala led not only to the data that made my study possible, but also to one of the first sketches of a local theology that I saw anywhere (1989). He has taken keen interest in this project and has always been most helpful in his suggestions. David Adeney, veteran China missionary and teacher, was likewise most generous in sharing his vast knowledge of the church in China. Professor Lorenzo Bautista of the Asian Theological Seminary in Manila put me in touch with crucial sources for a local theology of squatters; and Stanley Mutunga, a Ph.D. student at Fuller's School of World Mission, was most helpful in collecting stories from among his own Akamba people. Treve Johnson deserves thanks for helping me clarify my project, first as a student, then as a colleague, as he collected stories from a church group in Northern California; and Rob Cahill at Fuller for help in preparing the appendices. I must also acknowledge the interest and encouragement of Richard Mouw my colleague at Fuller who read parts of the manuscript, and of Robert K. Johnston of North Park Seminary who kept after me until I knew what I was trying to say in the introductory chapters.

But it is the people themselves who are so anxious to tell about the things they have seen and heard that are the most important colleagues in a study of this kind. Though they are nameless in this discussion they are known to God, and telling their stories is a part of the way all of us grow up into Christ in all things (Eph. 4:13–14). All of this goes to show that theological reflection, like a people's theology, is the work of many people walking along together as they seek to follow Christ in this present evil world. May this brief study encourage God's people to feel more deeply and live out more consistently the joyful reality of the Gospel.

Pasadena, California
October 1991

WORKS CITED

Robert Banks.
 1987.   *All the Business of Life: Bringing Theology Down to Earth.* Sutherland, NSW, Australia: Albatross.
Robert Bellah, Richard Masden, William M. Sullivan, Ann Swidler, and Steven M. Tipton.
 1985.   *Habits of the Heart: Individualism and Commitment in American Life.* Berkeley: University of California.
David Scotchmer.
 1989.   "Symbols of Salvation: A Local Mayan Protestant Theology" *Missiology.* 17/3:293–310.
Robert Schreiter.
 1985.   *Constructing Local Theologies.* Maryknoll: Orbis.
Robert Wuthnow.
 1991.   *Acts of Compassion: Caring for Others and Helping Ourselves.* Princeton: Princeton University.

Introduction

Chapter 1

Introduction: Toward
a Theology of the People

THE IMPLICATIONS OF THE CHURCH
AS AN INTER-CULTURAL BODY

The explosive growth of the church, especially in those areas of the world called the Third World, has enabled us to fill out John's vision in Revelation 7 in a very concrete way. There, you will remember, John sees a great multitude, that no one can number from every tribe and nation, singing praise to God. We know, for example, that that chorus will contain millions of Chinese Christians who worship in small house churches that up until recently were unnoticed by the powerful leaders of that nation. It will include many from the Indian peoples of Central America who are forced to scratch out a living from a tiny plot of land or to sell themselves to large multinationals as day laborers. Some, who presently make a precarious living on a large garbage dump in downtown Manila, Philippines, will join that chorus. Many will come from peoples of East Africa who at present are struggling with land that is losing its fertility and who are seeking to

14

preserve their cultural identity in the midst of modernizing forces they neither understand nor control. And, of course, there will be millions from North America who now rush off to work day by day via modern cars or light-rail systems while they struggle to maintain spiritual values in an often hostile environment.

Beyond the fact that Christians throughout the world face many kinds of difficulties, and often persecution, these images underline the diversity of issues that Christians are called to reflect upon today. Believers must not only wrestle with traditional problems of communicating the Gospel in the light of complex religious traditions, now they must reflect on entrenched racial prejudices, drug wars, complex political relationships, long-smoldering liberation movements, and all the problems associated with expanding city populations and the secularization of societies.

Beyond this, Christians now face a situation in which these realities are rapidly changing. Who would have dreamed that Eastern Europe would have experienced its liberation from Communism, or that South Africa would take steps to dismantle apartheid? Who can imagine what the political changes in China or the drug wars in Latin America will mean for the church in those places? Who could have imagined how quickly a crisis of the magnitude of the Gulf War could arise?

But for Christians concerned to see the church grow and prosper the real questions are: What shape will Christian obedience take in these places? And what kind of theological reflection is appropriate to this obedience? As a start to answering these questions we might begin by asking what kind of Christian thinking is already taking place there. How have Christians in these places understood the command to follow Christ?

Architects have a technical term for those structures that are designed and built by the people who will live in them. They call this vernacular architecture. For millennia people have taken whatever is at hand—rocks, mud, pieces of wood—to construct dwellings for themselves. On a world historical scale, of course, this has far and away been the most common kind of architecture, and even today produces structures of marvelous subtlety and beauty. In this study we would like to make a similar point for the kind of theology people commonly do as a part of their everyday lives. Let us think of this as *vernacular theology*: that theological framework constructed, often intuitively, by Christians seeking to respond faithfully to the challenges their lives present to them.

When things are put in this way it becomes immediately evident that a people's theology tends to respond to very specific and concrete issues. In China Christians ask: How does our faith in Christ relate to cooperation with the government-authorized Three-self Churches? For the Mam Indians, Christian reflection inevitably raises the question of their relation to the dominant Ladino culture. One of the discoveries of my previous study of Third-World theology was that systematic reflection outside the West tended to reflect much more on the actual social and even the economic situation of the people (Dyrness, 1990). And it tended to be much more mission oriented. In a word, it was closer to the real-life situations of people whose lives God had touched.

But while I found this exciting, when I finished those studies, I had the uneasy feeling that large parts of the church and large areas of experience were still being left out. After all, I was still only reading about people who had access to higher (usually Western) education and modern publishing facilities (and who wrote in one of the few languages I could read). What about the vast body of preachers and teachers who had no access to these things: What sort of theology were they doing?

During the year our family lived in Africa, and I was writing on Third-World theology, we occasionally visited the large independent church in Mathare Valley, Nairobi, called the Redeemed Gospel Church. There, each Sunday, several thousand believers crowded into a circus tent to hear Bishop Kitonga preach in English and Swahili. As I listened, I realized that I was hearing theology being done in an oral mode that communicated directly to the people living in this vast and sprawling slum settlement. The bishop regularly related biblical passages to the problems of drugs, thievery, and alcoholism. I began to urge my students to go and listen to the bishop and reflect on the theology he was doing.

From these experiences has grown an increasing conviction that there is an entire dimension of theological reflection that theologians regularly ignore, or even despise; theological frameworks that ordinary Christians develop in the course of their experiences with God and Scripture. I began to ask myself, How can we take advantage of this change in focus? What will the enterprise of theology look like in such a world? One answer that is commonly given (or assumed) is that it must continue to look like it has always looked. After all, God's Word cannot change, so the truth of Christianity and the Gospel will be the same—it will meet these new challenges in the same victorious way that it has met previous difficulties.

This point of view was reflected in the comment of a veteran missionary to Africa when he heard that I was writing a book about theology in the Third World. He was glad I was doing that, he said, because much that new Christians in Africa were writing and saying was wrong. We should encourage them, he concluded, but we need to be very careful to help them correct their mistakes.

On the one hand, I am sympathetic with this friend. I, too, am concerned when Christianity loses its unique character by being mixed with other religious systems. I, too, am concerned when God's activity is limited to liberation movements. But on the other hand, I reject the underlying attitude that this comment reflects. Quite apart from the fact that African Christians have no monopoly on bad theology, this attitude reflects the misconception that good theology has already been discovered and developed (usually in the context of Western Christianity), and it needs only to be exported and taught in Third World training schools. As I heard one theologian mistakenly put it recently, in doing cross-cultural theology we do not need to "reinvent the wheel."

This thinking ignores two facts. First, Western theology is itself a reflection of its Western cultural and historical setting, and therefore cannot possibly meet the needs of the vastly different settings of Third World churches—though it certainly may contribute to theological reflection in those settings. Second, as we have seen, these churches are working on special problems that are inescapably a part of their theological reflection, and, since we are beginning to understand that these issues are also of great significance for us, their Christian and biblical reflection will be essential for us. It might even be that their reflection, rooted as it is in the tough concerns of everyday life, might contribute to the renewal of theological reflection in our own setting. Let us deal with these two realities in some detail.

First, theology in the West has developed under unique historical circumstances. The issues here are very complex, but we might summarize things in this way. A particular understanding of the Gospel, and therefore of the discipline of theology, has grown up in the West under the influence of Greek philosophy and our interaction with that philosophy. There have been attempts from time to time to purify our understanding and practice of the Gospel from alien influence—revival and reform movements have been common in the history of Christianity, but even these attempts have borne the mark of their intellectual milieu.

Two-hundred years ago this heritage coalesced in a cultural and intellectual movement called the Enlightenment, which celebrated liberty, reason, and the progress and perfectibility of human society. To defend themselves against the atheism and agnosticism that threatened to take over this movement, Christians sought to define a "reasonable Christianity" that reflected these challenges. Robert Schreiter has characterized the theological method that developed as the search for "sure knowledge" of God and his truth (1985:88 and cf. Lesslie Newbigin, 1989:3–7).

This tradition has sought to give a critical, rational account of faith using the tools of a discipline that can offer the most exact form of knowledge known to our culture. Because our culture values reason and the scientific method, these have become the preferred tools for theological inquiry. In our century the disciplines of the social sciences have been added to the theologian's bag of tricks, but the goal remains the same: The knowledge gained must be first, and foremost, *sure.*

The essence of theology, then, has to do with what can be thought and explained with precision and certainty. The philosopher Plato played an important role in this when he insisted that truth has to do with an ideal and timeless realm, and the goal of human life is to acquire knowledge of that reality and live according to the truth discovered. René Descartes, a famous precursor of the Enlightenment, also played a role in his search for clear and distinct ideas.

This development also has much to do with the particularities of our cultural history, especially since the Reformation. There, the communal and imaginatively rich world of the middle ages was exchanged for the precision of Christian preaching and teaching. John Bossy believes that this change was, at least in part, a social and cultural change. The ritualistic and fraternal world of public Mass and frequent feasts of the medieval period was replaced by private meditation and reflection after the Reformation. With the development of printing, educational levels began to rise and the private piety (what came to be called personal faith) of the average believer was emphasized. Ministry, Bossy says, came to be understood as moral supervision, which led to modern individualistic and private interpretations of faith (1985).

Increasingly the major challenges to Christianity were addressed to this conception of theology as certain and precise knowledge and individual practice. Since the time of Descartes, for example, doubt has become a major apologetic issue. The question has been how competing bodies of knowledge—scientific, and more recently, sociological and anthropological—relate to the body of knowledge known as theology. A vast apologetic industry arose that sought to defend this conception of faith from these epistemological attacks. The question we want to raise here is not whether these are real challenges, clearly they are. But are these the challenges that Christians in other places must also face?

This has clearly been the operating assumption in most missionary-training schools. Fresh from skirmishes along these battle lines, missionaries, upon arrival in Manila or Nairobi, mounted the same artillery and dressed their students in the same armor they had used at home. The response however was often not what they expected. I still remember the puzzlement of my well-educated Filipino friends to the arguments of Francis Schaeffer in the 1970s—arguments that I had found exciting and convincing. The problems of true truth and personal meaning made no impact on their intuitive group-oriented consciousness.

At the very least, a general haze came to settle over the study of theology and apologetics when it was imported from abroad. Students dutifully took notes and wrote exams, but went home to their villages, where children continued to die young and crops sometimes refused to grow, with no clear idea of how to reflect biblically on these things. Under the worse circumstances, there ensued what Kenyan novelist Ngugi Wa Thiong'o calls a "colonization of the mind." In this situation African (or Asian or Latin American) students are made to dress up as Hamlet and King Lear (or, in our case, as Carl Henry or Rudolf Bultmann) and imagine they are discovering the world. What Ngugi said of the study of literature applies with equal validity to theology. As we studied, he says, "language and literature were taking us further and further from ourselves to other selves, from our world to other worlds" (1986:12).

Under particular influences, then, theological truth in the West has come to be identified with knowledge that can be expressed in propositional form and defended with great critical skill. Clearly the resources this tradition has given us, especially in the areas of historical reconstruction and critical analysis, have proven invaluable to Christian thought. But the question we raise here is whether this method is the only way in which thinking about God can be carried out, and, even more pointedly, whether we might not have something to learn from other ways of thinking about God.

This brings us to the second reality we noted above: Christian communities outside the West are rapidly reaching a maturity and visibility that demands attention and respect. Christians in Africa now outnumber those in the North America (by 212 million to 187 million), and are increasing at a rate of sixteen thousand every day. The underground house-church movement in China may number twenty to thirty million. Moreover these churches are struggling, with increasing sophistication, with issues that are of growing concern to us as well. This has resulted in bold attempts to think about Christianity in new ways. I have reviewed some of these discussions in a previous book, and alluded to them at the beginning of this chapter. But let me outline some of them briefly here.

Christians in sub-Saharan Africa have been called to reexamine their cultural and historical identity in the face of their colonial past and the resurgence of African traditional religions. With rapidly growing churches and a shortage of trained leaders, Christians struggle to relate their faith to their past in a way that preserves both their Christian and their African identities. In South Africa Christians face strong practices and habits that have encouraged the separate development of the races. Christians have often been caught in the middle of virulent debates between extremists on both sides as they seek to pursue justice.

Similarly, in Latin America a history of oppression has resulted in societies characterized by widespread and entrenched injustices. Christians there have tried to think about their faith and read Scripture from the point of view of those suffering such abuses. This has raised far-reaching questions

that, according to many observers, is revising—or threaten-
ing—the very nature of biblical faith.

In Asia, strong religious and philosophical traditions put
entirely different issues on the table. In some cases Christians
have been tempted to compromise the uniqueness of Christianity in the light of these traditions. In all events believers
are called on to reexamine biblical uniqueness in the light of
Hindu or Buddhist beliefs.

These discussions, like those in the West, reflect the
unique culture and history of those places. These settings
raise other questions than that of sure knowledge, or, to put
the issue more precisely, they put the epistemological discussions in wholly different and problematic contexts. They have
raised such questions as the following: What is the way to real
human development? What role does liberal democracy play
in this? Or, what is the role of Western-style capitalism? What
of the people's identity in all this? How do they take charge of
their own future in the light of large and sometimes menacing
political and economic powers?

Clearly, there is much to lose by ignoring the theological
reflection that is taking place in these vigorous communities—just as they would be impoverished if they ignored all
that has been learned in Western Christianity. But we may put
the matter in an even more pointed way: There is a particular
sense that theological reflection in the West badly needs
renewal. Though the Western tradition has developed great
sophistication in issues of methodology, what has come to be
broadly called hermeneutics, it has done less well with issues
ordinary lay Christians wrestle with. What we have gained in
clarity, in other words, we have sometimes lost in immediacy
and emotional depth—the theological knowledge we have
gained has sometimes become estranged from everyday life.
Recently Bernard Cooke has argued, for example, that the
reality of God in Western thinking has grown increasingly
distant. While in the first decades of Christianity there was a
natural intimacy with God and a naturalness of faith, this was
increasingly mediated in various ways until God the Father

became a stranger (1990). A fresh intimacy with God is clearly one of the gifts to the church of much lay theological reflection coming from around the world.

The question that we address in this book is the following: Does all this suggest a different way (or many different ways) of doing theology? We cannot propose any definitive answer to this question in this book but we can begin to show the ways the question may be raised. In particular we can ask how it is possible to begin a conversation between those coming from very different settings so that we might be put in a position to learn from one another?

We are using theology in a way that calls for very careful definition—a major task for the remainder of this chapter. But before turning to this task, it is necessary to review the importance of social science in all of this.

THE TOOLS OF SOCIOLOGISTS AND ANTHROPOLOGISTS

We have already noted that a major factor in the received understanding of theology in the West has been the philosophical tradition coming from Plato. The influence of this tradition has played a major role in the growing elaboration of theology as "sure knowledge." Now it would be foolish to see this development as entirely wrong-headed. Indeed were we to make a detailed critique of its strengths and weaknesses—something beyond the scope of this book—it would be with the conceptual tools that this theological heritage has bequeathed us. Nor is it wise to conclude that this tradition has no value for the theology of the developing world—an impossible assumption in any case given the dominance of Western-educated professors in Third-World universities and seminaries.

But two things temper our enthusiasm for the Western tradition of theology. First, broad rethinking within the Western intellectual tradition over the past two-hundred years has changed the way we are apt to discuss sure knowledge. Beginning with the Danish philosopher Søren Kierkegaard, social and even emotional factors have increasingly been seen to play an important role in the way we shape our knowledge. Further, the influence of thinkers in the tradition of Immanuel Kant and Wilhelm Dilthey have shown us that knowledge is, at least in part, an interpretation of reality, so that the knowledge we have of things will ordinarily reflect our special assumptions about the world. These in turn relate to our own cultural and historical location. More recently, historians of Christianity are making use of social-science method to show the cultural influences on the development of Christian thought and institutions—one thinks of Peter Brown on the early church and John Bossy on the Reformation. Though I will not attempt to do so here, it could be argued that even these developments have not substantially changed the way theology as sure knowledge is being written and discussed in the West, at least among evangelicals.

But there is a further related development that has influenced our evaluation of traditional Western theology: the increasing prominence of social-science method. Paralleling the developments sketched above has been the growing maturation of the disciplines of sociology and anthropology. In the former, especially in what has come to be called the sociology of knowledge, we are coming to a progressively clearer understanding of the importance and influence of our social setting on our lives and even on our thinking processes (Berger and Luckmann, 1967).

But for our purposes the recent work of anthropologists is of even greater significance. These writers are helping us understand the details of the social setting in which we find ourselves, and in and through which we Christians live out and understand our faith. Clifford Geertz, for example, has pioneered an understanding of culture as "webs of meaning" in which people locate themselves. His definition of culture will be important for us throughout our study so it is worth quoting at length:

[Culture is] an historically transmitted pattern of meaning, embodied in symbols, a system of inherited conceptions expressed in symbolic forms, by means of which [people] communicate, perpetuate and develop their knowledge about and attitudes toward life (1973:89).

Notice the emphasis is on seeing culture as a growing pattern of meaning, accumulating over time. Therefore a culture has to be put within an historical setting to be properly understood. Moreover it consists in symbols—language, ritual events, practices—that express the meaning people use to orient themselves in the world and communicate among each other.

Geertz speaks of an analysis of culture, using Gilbert Ryle's term, as "thick description" (1973:3–30). That is, for example, apparently insignificant gestures, such as contracting one's eyelid, must be understood in terms of larger patterns of social meaning—winking to a co-conspirator. Obviously these meanings can only be clearly understood from the inside, from the actor's point of view, and other constructions, as outsiders, will always be tentative—they will be an interpretation. But the advantage of such interpretive sketches, as Geertz points out in another place, is that an outsider can sometimes extend the insider's interpretation of reality. An outsider, by tracing the larger curve of social discourse—what is being "said" by a people, can sometimes reshape categories so they can "reach beyond the contexts in which they originally arose. . .so as to locate affinities and mark differences" (1983:12). We cannot become a "native," but we can converse with them, and they with us. The converse of this is that we can more accurately (and more modestly) begin to see ourselves, and our culture, as a case among cases.

What is the significance of this view of culture for understanding religion? Religious discussion is obviously a special case, however rooted in cultural realities it may be. Geertz, in a now classic article, attempts to describe religion in the form of a symbolic system (1973:87–125). Religion is, he says, a system of symbols that acts to establish powerful, pervasive, and long-lasting moods and motivations in people by formulating conceptions of a general order of existence, and clothing these conceptions with such an aura of factuality that the mood and motivations seem uniquely realistic. Religious symbols, like the cross worn by Christians, "store" meanings that "sum up. . .what is known about the way the world is, the quality of the emotional life it supports, and the way one ought to behave while in it" (Ibid., 127).

Notice first that elements of the common-sense world, are said, by means of this symbolic system, to find a larger context in this wider world. Common life is moreover, corrected and completed by this larger world. When African Christians begin their letters by bringing greetings to brothers and sisters in the strong name of Jesus, they are not simply adding pious touches to their communication. They are expressing something fundamental about their view of reality. Symbols, then, are expressed through ritual acts and practices that do not so much represent faith, as present or portray it. Symbols, rituals, confessions of faith, and religious behavior must all be understood in a single web of meaning that makes up religion. These meanings furthermore include not only explicit statements of belief or particular symbols, but also common practices that develop over time.

Christians have not always been eager to make use of the language and methods of anthropologists, sometimes for good reason. It is not hard to argue that naturalistic assumptions have influenced much of the theory of contemporary social science. A sociologist who has recently argued this way is Stan Gaede. Among social scientists today, he argues, "Only [the naturalist] is given the freedom and privilege of complete integrity, where personal and professional assumptions coincide" (1985:57). While these issues are too complex to discuss in detail here, the following observations may be helpful.

First, there is surely evidence in support of Gaede's claim. In one place for example, Geertz contends that any description of religion must avoid either the point of view of the atheist or the preacher. Beliefs must be allowed to appear in a clear neutral light. For it belongs to the "power of the scientific imagination to bring us into touch with the lives of strangers" (1973:16). There are questions that remain, he admits, such as whether religious experience or claims can be genuine or true. But these questions cannot even be asked "within the self-imposed limitations of the scientific perspective" (Ibid., 123). That is to say, questions of truth or falsity are not unimportant, they simply cannot be answered by anthropologists. Their goal is the more limited one of observing the culturally other so as to understand them.

Peter Berger, a sociologist who is also a Christian, calls this position, which he himself endorses, "methodological atheism" (1969:100). This position of neutrality is necessary for the sociologist because, he says, within the scientific frame of reference religious projections can only be dealt with as human products. Rigorous brackets must be placed around the question of whether these projections refer to something real.

The Christian, understandably, has problems with this restriction. For as Gregory Baum says in his excellent discussion of these things, Geertz's—and apparently Berger's—description of religion leaves out two essential components of any genuine faith. First, understanding religion as a "symbolic system" makes no allowance for the sacred in religion. That is in limiting discussion to human projections there is no allowance for the actual appearance of God. Second, it follows that distinctly religious experience, that is direct experience of God himself, is left out of account. On any analysis of religion these elements are surely central to the "symbolic meaning" (1975:254).

Inherent in any sociological description is the danger of "reductionism," that is reducing a reality to its observable dimension. In this case it appears that the atheism of Émile Durkheim, who was influential in these developments of the sociology of religion, has limited what counts as proper description. If God does not exist, religion must be explained apart from the divine. But, the Christian responds, if God does exist, can it leave the divine presence out of account? It appears, Baum insists, that the danger is not simply in misrepresenting the religious dimension, but also in foregoing resources that are ready to hand in describing and explaining religion. Is the faith of the sociologist of no use in the investigation? Clearly it is. Baum concludes: "The faith of sociologists that a religious tradition expresses something of the divine creates a special sensitivity to this religion, a greater awareness of its hidden meanings, and above all a sense of its forward movement. I find the ontological agnosticism recommended by Peter Berger difficult to visualize" (1975:262).

But the question remains: Why can't a believer take the descriptive method of Geertz or Berger and use it within the context of faith? Baum not only insists that this is possible, but goes so far as to say that theology, in this case, can result in "a critical prolongation of sociological concepts" (1975:-263).

Before we turn to the implications of this for theology, let us consider the understanding of theory that has emerged in the work of Geertz, to see whether we might have something to learn from his discussion. Formulation of theory—"systematic modes of assessment" (1973:24)—Geertz admits, is difficult for an "interpretive view"—as his position is characterized. Ordinarily we gain understanding by inspecting actual events, not by "arranging abstracted entities into unified patterns" (Ibid., 16). But aren't such patterns precisely what we mean by theory? And by extension, we will ask, aren't such patterns of behavior and biblical truth what we mean by Christian theology? Is not theology the orderly presentation of our experience, belief, and understanding of God?

The difficulty is, for an interpretive view that depends in large part on description, theory must relate to actual events and practices, it must stand closer to the ground than in other sciences (1973:24). If it is unseverable from the thick description to which it relates, how does one generalize? The answer, Geertz insists, is that one has to generalize within, and not across, cases. One makes, he says, clinical inferences (Ibid.:25). One does not, in other words, begin with a set of observations and try to subsume them under a general law. Rather one looks for key signifiers in the case being observed and places them within an intelligible frame.

Rather than trying to make predictions about cultural activity, one tries to elaborate from the meaning the events have for the participants, knowledge about the society in question and indeed about social life as such (1973:27). This means that theory for Geertz is meant to provide a vocabulary in which the meaning of the larger symbolic world can be expressed. "The essential vocation of interpretive anthropology is not to answer our deepest questions, but to make available to us answers that others. . .have given and thus to include them in the consultable record of what [people] have said" (Ibid., 30).

We are going to argue that this way of opening conversation among cultures has great implication for the way theological discussion can proceed. With the qualifications we have made, these categories can help us develop the skills of listening across cultural boundaries, so that we can make available to the church worldwide a broader record of what Christians believe and what God is doing in our day. We might even begin to make "clinical inferences," in which shared experiences produce a more nuanced understanding of our own faith.

A NEW DIMENSION TO THE STUDY OF THEOLOGY: VERNACULAR THEOLOGY

With these tools in hand we are ready to turn to the question: What is theology? Can we define it in a way so that our theological and cultural traditions can make use of the tools provided by the social sciences? Can such an understanding of theology moreover be cross-culturally valid?

We are assuming in this study that Scripture as a Word

from God is the cross-culturally valid element in Christian theology. But the contents of Scripture come in terms of the particular biblical cultures. Of course the Gospel or Good News always relates in some way to God's love revealed in the life, death, and resurrection of Christ, but the element of the Gospel that strikes one as being good may vary according to cultural perceptions—is it forgiveness of sins? release from spiritual bondage? union with God? or is it food for my family or returning home after exile? What we find in Scripture is a variety of ways in which this Good News is expressed, usually relating very specifically—as in Paul's letters—to some historical and social situation. All of the many images for redemption for example—freedom from slavery, deliverance from evil powers, turning from idols to the living God—add richness to our conception of the salvation Christ brought. Now, if we find in Scripture that the setting for the most profound revelation of God's truth is the concrete experience of God's people, we should not be surprised if today that truth was apprehended similarly in the concrete lives of believers.

One of the encouraging factors in current theological discussion is the growing recognition of the derivative character of theological discussion. Daniel Van Allmen more than a decade ago argued in an important article that in the New Testament the life and worship of the community is the primary thing. Theology comes along later to provide an ordering function (1975). Paul Holmer acknowledged in *The Grammar of Faith* (1978) that the theologian has no special organ, she is a debtor to what is primary—Scripture and the lives and thought of the faithful. "God's ways are still discovered by his friends and not in virtue of techniques and agencies of power" (Ibid., 22). Nancey Murphy at the conclusion of her study of the status of contemporary theological discourse argues that "theology is a rational reconstruction of the beliefs of the Christian community. Its job is to examine the community's belief system in order to display the relations among its parts and its justification relative to whatever else there is" (1990:196). Therefore the actual knowledge of God, she says, begins with the amateurs not with the theologians (Ibid.).

The importance of this point can hardly be overemphasized. Often it is said that this or that group "has no theology." Now if this is taken to mean that this community has written no theological treatise, or has no theologically trained spokespeople, then it may be accurate. But if it is meant to imply this community has no framework or systematic understanding of their faith, it is clearly false.

Here again we must guard against the assumption that theology must be clear and articulated knowledge. For most people in the world (and indeed for many Americans), whose formal education may be minimal, the notion of theology as abstract knowledge is simply unhelpful. We are working with the assumption that faith involves a web, or framework, of symbols in terms of which people make choices about what is important to them. Now it is a mistake, Charles Taylor reminds us, to assume that because people operate without a philosophically defined framework, they have no framework at all. This is a hazardous assumption, for many people live lives "entirely structured by supremely important qualitative distinctions in relation to which they literally live and die" (1990:21), but who could not describe these distinctions in any comprehensive way. Most people live, and all of us live at times, with values and commitments that cannot be fully articulated. This does not keep them from motivating us, and it certainly does not exempt them from being subject to critical evaluation.

A theological framework ordinarily operates in this way—it becomes a part of the tacit knowledge by which we live our lives. Now it is certainly true that a clearer understanding of one's beliefs is part of what it means to become a mature Christian. At the Reformation, one of John Calvin's contributions was to question the notion that a vague faith in the church—what Catholic theology calls implicit faith—was sufficient for salvation. He insisted this was only another name for ignorance. But many people in the West take this to mean that growth in knowledge is all there is to Christian maturity. This is part of the problem with our assumption that a framework is primarily of abstract knowledge. To show the weakness of this, it is enough to point out how easy it is to give full intellectual assent to a belief that we deny by our behavior.

By a framework we mean a symbolic complex of ideas, objects, events (cf. ritual and nonritual acts), and language that both express and define what we mean by Christianity. The system we have in mind could well be described by Alasdair MacIntyre's notion of a "practice," which is "any coherent and complex form of socially established cooperative human activity through which goods. . .are realized in the course of trying to achieve those standards of excellence which are appropriate to, and partially definitive of, that form of activity" (1984:187). Notice that the significance of this practice, what we might call Christian living, lies in its interactive character, as well as in the conjunction of activities and standards, and in its orientation toward what is conceived as the good, (helping one's neighbor in distress as a means of showing the glory of God).

What is key to a community's framework, what we might call its implicit theology, may as well be found in a practice as in the dominant ideas it espouses. Take, for example, the singing of spirituals in an African-American church. One might analyze the lyrics of these songs to discover the theology of these people. But if this were done in isolation from the manner in which the songs are actually used in worship or in the home, or in isolation from the sense of alienation blacks feel outside this arena as compared with the belonging they feel inside, it would be positively misleading. A close reading of black singing may well show them to be, in Schreiter's term, paradigms of thought in the culture that might express a depth of meaning otherwise unavailable (1985:78).

We might even put the goal this way: Theological reflection is meant to take us deeper into our everyday lives and probe these for the meaning of our faith, to see whether our practice really reflects what we say we believe about God. For, as Clifford Geertz reminds us, symbols and beliefs that mark the religious life express "their meaning [in] the role they play in an ongoing pattern of life not from any intrinsic relationships they bear to one another" (1973:17).

METHOD OF DOING THEOLOGY
WITH THE PEOPLE

Let us review our progress. We began by acknowledging that the presence and complexity of a world-wide church has given us the opportunity to rethink how theology can be done at the end of the twentieth century. Not only has it put new issues on the theological agenda, but it has forced us to take a new, critical look at our own received ideas about theology.

The sense of cultural and historical diversity this review gives suggests we employ new tools of description and analysis that social scientists (and some recent philosophers) have given us. We found these helpful—especially Clifford Geertz's idea of religion as a complex symbolic system, but observed that these tools may reflect naturalistic assumptions and must be used critically. Further, we have seen that theological reflection needs to include the practices of Christian communities as well as their verbal or written statements. Lastly, we have redrawn the function of theology as generalizing within, rather than across cases—as working on the whole symbolic complex of a community's Christian life so as to distill a vocabulary in which its meaning can be described, shared, and then valued. The result of this kind of descriptive analysis we have described as a vernacular theology.

As we have noticed in most discussions of theology the people of God are as silent as they are invisible. As Brazilian Bishop Helder Camara once said, there is a profound difference between working for the people and working with the people.

Theologians, as well as development workers, could well take this to heart. As in development, which seeks not simply to feed people, but to give them skills to take charge of their lives, so what we are after is a theological discipline that empowers people to be the people of God. We must seek to enable them to read and obey Scripture for themselves. If there is one generalization that could be made about the Gospel across cultures, it is that it is God's means of delivering people from all kinds of bondage and leading them to enjoy the freedom appropriate to his children.

The process we are describing, then, is meant to give the people their voice. The outsider is placed in the modest but critical role of a sympathetic listener to these stories of faith, even, at some points, as a participant observer in their Christian practices. This provides the dimension of theological reflection we have called descriptive and interpretive.

But a major question now emerges. How does this descriptive function relate to the normative and critical function ordinarily assigned to theology? The answer to this may be given in two ways. First, there is a sense that the only valid critique of theological practice must be internal. That is, contrary to the advice of my friend in Africa, Western theologians, while they may point out problems, ultimately cannot provide the critical perspective that African theology needs. That perspective needs to be formed from within the African church.

Not that outsiders have no role to play; indeed I will argue that a major function of the dialogue between different local theologies is the critique that they provide for one another. But often this critique is convincing not because it represents a better theory (i.e., a more convincing or rationally defensible point of view), but because it embodies a better set of practices. We often say that what people do speaks so loud that we cannot hear what they say. What this really means is that the power of righteousness (or of evil) in one's life carries a conviction that often surpasses mere verbal argumentation. Similarly an encounter by the Western church of the joy of

Chinese believers, the anguish of Latin Americans, or the eager anticipation of God's deliverance by Africans, can provide a critical function for our Western theology.

The second way to answer the question about the relation between descriptive and normative theology is to make a distinction between these as differing dimensions of doing theology. A major part of Christian growth is unconscious and unnoticed—we grow from the nourishment of worship and fellowship just as we naturally grow by eating the right kinds of physical foods. In a sense, even on this level, the Gospel is doing a "critical" work; it is shaping and molding the people who obey it, but this is often largely unconscious and its meaning unarticulated. Being unconscious and unarticulated does not mean that this growth is without theological significance. Indeed, for most people, and for all of us some of the time, theological reflection is commonly done in this informal way.

Here is where the sympathetic listening of outsiders becomes important. I believe that encouraging people to articulate and defend what they believe—by simply allowing them to tell their stories—is a first step, not only in Christian growth, but in more self-conscious and critical theological reflection. Giving them a voice is a necessary prerequisite to allowing them to be dialogue partners either with us or with the major voices of Christian tradition. Students who take the time to listen and reflect on a people's testimonies frequently report how important this turns out to be for the people they interview.

From these experiences I have become convinced that we have typically put things in reverse order in our theological education. In our zeal to get people to reflect theologically we pull out the largest artillery, insisting they read Calvin and Barth before they have any notion what theology is, or how they really feel about God. Instead we ought to take the time to help people understand what their own (sometimes hidden) assumptions about faith and salvation are, and only then put them in conversation with what others in their traditions (or in other traditions) have said about these things.

Obviously there will come a time when descriptive theology will give way to more self-consciously critical theology. The critical perspective may be provided in two ways. Most commonly, as I have said, it comes through the encounter with a superior set of practices, through the impact of power, either of healing or of a righteous life. This concrete critical perspective may be illustrated by the parables of Jesus or by the vision of liberation in Latin American theology. But a critical perspective may also be provided by abstract conceptions, by theoretical considerations that seek to discipline thought and action. Most Western theology, of course, is of this kind. Here the practices and beliefs of a community are submitted to the discipline of particular categories—as when we say that abortion is wrong because it violates the Christian conception of human creation in the image of God.

While we recognize the importance of this critical ordering role of theology, this will not be a major aspect of the present study. Our role here is more modest. We will be working on that first—descriptive and interpretive—level in which the skills of listening and understanding are paramount. Within each chapter, and especially in the conclusion, we will make some start toward developing critical perspectives with these materials, but this will be done in a very tentative way.

We have chosen five communities from various parts of the world to examine: the House Church in China; Mam Indians in Guatemala; Christians from a squatter settlement in Manila; Akamba Christians in Kenya, East Africa; and finally American middle-class believers from Northern California. We want to make some start toward developing a local or vernacular theology of these people.

Our work will be to first make some observations about the social, historical, and cultural setting in which these communities live. This aspect is sometimes limited by the resources available and the author's capacities, but it is included to emphasize that a grasp of cultural realities at some level is essential to understand a developing theology. What collection of cultural themes has emerged as being centrally important? These might involve the relationship of time and the passage of time, and the meaning ascribed to these by members of this cultural group, as well as the Christians among them. Or, they might relate to the relationship of the person to the community and to the larger world. Finally, there may be questions relating to the mediation of power, or of interaction with the spiritual world.

These cultural values will ordinarily be described from the point of view of adherents of traditional religions. Following this, and against this backdrop, we will describe the complex of faith and practices that have developed in the Christian community. The method will be to seek to describe a number of key symbols and explain their meaning for the people, as far as possible, in their own words. For this reason the preferred source material is the narrative of conversion, or of some crisis experience in which God intervened. Narratives provide a more genuine picture of a people's faith than do more objective modes, as people tend to "own" their stories more than they do abstract descriptions. A corollary of this is that a people's actual theology as it is practiced is not the same as they might claim that it is.

The purpose is to provide for these believers and for ourselves a clearer picture of what God is doing among them, and to develop a vocabulary to describe the meaning of this activity. By this diversity of reflection (and interpretation) of the Gospel we might be able to see our theologies as commentaries on one another, "the one lighting what the other darkens" (Geertz, 1983:233).

WORKS CITED

Gregory Baum.
  1975.   *Religion and Alienation: A Theological Reading of Sociology.* New York: Paulist.
Peter Berger.
  1969.   *The Sacred Canopy: Elements of a Sociological Theory of Religion.* Garden City: Anchor.
Peter Berger and Thomas Luckmann.
  1967.   *The Social Construction of Reality: A Treatise in the Sociology of Knowledge.* Garden City: Anchor.
John Bossy.
  1985.   *Christianity in the West: 1400–1700.* Oxford: Oxford University.
Peter Brown.
  1982.   *Society and the Holy in Late Antiquity.* London: Faber and Faber.
Bernard Cooke.
  1990.   *The Distancing of God.* Minneapolis: Augsburg/Fortress.
William Dyrness.
  1990.   *Learning About Theology from the Third World.* Grand Rapids: Zondervan.
Stanley D. Gaede.
  1985.   *Where Gods May Dwell: On Understanding the Human Condition.* Grand Rapids: Zondervan.
Clifford Geertz.
  1973.   *Interpretation of Cultures.* New York: Basic.

———.
  1983.   *Local Knowledge: Further Essays in Interpretive Culture.* New York: Basic.
Paul Holmer.
  1978.   *The Grammar of Faith.* San Francisco: Harper and Row.
Nancey Murphy.
  1990.   *Theology in the Age of Scientific Reasoning.* Ithaca: Cornell University.

Alasdair MacIntyre.
    1984.   *After Virtue*. 2d ed. South Bend: University of Notre Dame.

Lesslie Newbigin.
    1989.   *The Gospel in a Pluralistic Society*. Grand Rapids: Eerdmans.

Ngugi Wa Thiong'O.
    1986.   *Decolonizing the Mind: The Politics of Language in African Literature*. Nairobi: Heinemann Kenya.

Robert J. Schreiter.
    1985.   *Constructing Local Theologies*. Maryknoll: Orbis.

Charles Taylor.
    1990.   *Sources of the Self: The Making of Modern Identity*. Cambridge, Mass.: Harvard University.

Daniel Van Allmen.
    1975.   "The Birth of Theology." *International Review of Missions*. 44:37–55.

China

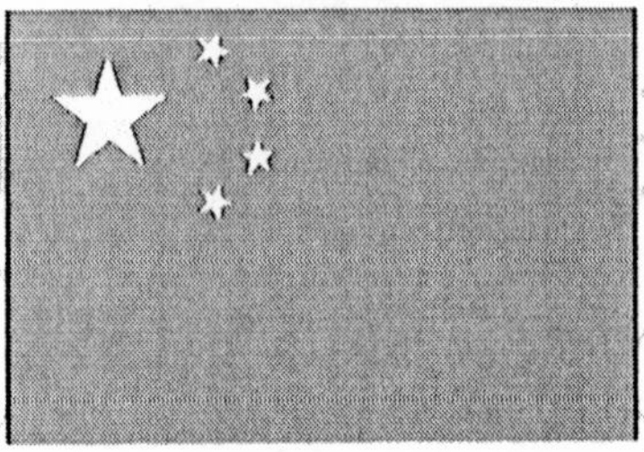

Chapter 2

The Theology of the House Churches in China

HISTORICAL AND CULTURAL CONTEXT

China, with its three millennia of history and rich cultural heritage, is home to more than one billion people, a staggering one quarter of the world's population. Since deserts, mountains and grasslands make up more than 90 percent of the area, China's vast population must be fed from the 7 percent of the land that is arable. Indeed during the fifty years in which its population has doubled, China's agricultural lands have decreased drastically—thirty million acres have been lost in just the last twenty years.

As the government works to feed its people, it also wrestles with how much freedom to allow and what contacts to encourage with the outside world. After the wrenching events associated with the 1989 uprising in Tiananmen Square, no one can be sure about what is happening in China today, especially where Christianity is concerned. But it is safe to say that major struggles continue to relate to China's need to develop in order to care for its people, as this is complicated by its ambiguous relationship to the outside world. As contemporary political swings continue to demonstrate, the Chinese people have never been able to free themselves either from a deep suspicion of, or a wide ranging curiosity about, foreign people and cultures.

Christianity, from the beginning of its introduction into China, has been caught in the tension created by this ambiguity. While Christians like Matteo Ricci (1552–1610) were sometimes welcomed as bearers of the advances of Western culture, their religion was often dismissed as a foreign entity. Indeed missionaries, especially in the nineteenth century, often compounded the difficulty by their cultural insensitivity. There were exceptions—Hudson Taylor was the most notable—but these were exceptions that proved the rule. In 1868, in fact, this founder of the China Inland Mission (which had begun in 1865) had this to say about Christianity in China

> The foreign appearance of the chapels and indeed the foreign air given to everything connected with religion have very largely hindered the rapid dissemination of the truth among the Chinese. But why need such a foreign aspect be given to Christianity? The Word of God does not require it; nor I conceive would reason justify it (quoted in Adeney, 39).

During a century torn apart by opium wars and dynastic decline some rulers recognized the importance of Western contacts for the development of China; others, often concurrently, were stirring up the people to drive out foreigners. Finally events culminated in the notorious Boxer Rebellion in which the Manchu rulers unofficially supported a movement that killed thousands of Chinese Christians and some 250 missionaries.

These tensions manifested themselves again in the struggle between the traditionalists and the modernists at the beginning of this century. Some Chinese sought to preserve the traditional Buddhist and Confucian faiths; others dismissed these as superstitions and embraced the thoughts of

John Dewey and Charles Darwin. Interestingly the goal of both embodied the traditional Chinese "pursuit of a nobler, more peaceful, more abundant, more harmonious, more perfect and longer life" (Lam, 20). The influence of traditional faiths has been a constant throughout Chinese history, and, if anything, is growing today. Many Chinese read the *Analects* of Confucius (551–483 B.C.E.) in school and at home, and its values of benevolence and filial piety figure largely in the Chinese imagination. Likewise Buddhism exerts an influence, especially in its emphasis on meditation and sudden enlightenment. These traditions along with others have contributed to the tendency to introspection so prominent among educated Chinese and to an emphasis on human efforts for self-improvement. These are rich and admirable traditions and Christianity has often been despised because it seems to lack the philosophical sophistication of these "Chinese" religions. At the same time a strong, popular belief in spirits, and the continuing influence of ancestors who must be appeased by appropriate sacrifice continues to flourish among the people— especially the peasants. As one Christian testified, "In the countryside, activities of the devil and the evil spirits were plenty" (quoted in Chao, 1988:65).

Though the intellectuals supported the 1911 revolution, Sun Zhong-shan (who was a Christian) was not able to control the whole country. After the Bolshevik revolution (in 1917), and the humiliation of the Versailles settlement, many intellectuals became disillusioned with the West and looked to Russia, and to Marx and Lenin, for guidance. Under the leadership of Mao Zedong the Communists progressively consolidated their power until they were able to defeat nationalist armies after World War II (1945–1949).

THE CHURCH IN CHINA

In 1900 Protestant churches claimed a membership of 113,000 with 1,600 Chinese Christian workers and two thousand mission̶ ̶̶ ̶ ̶ey, 41). In 1949 the figure reached probably 1.5 mi̶ ̶̶ ̶ ̶nd the most conservative estimates today put the ̶ ̶̶ ̶er at five to six million (with an equal number of R̶c̶ ̶ ̶ ̶Catholics). But a more accurate figure, if the undergro̶ ̶ ̶house churches are taken into account, may be anywher̶ ̶ ̶tween twenty and fifty million. How can this explosion ̶ ̶rowth be accounted for?

Dur̶ ̶ ̶the early part of the century, as we noticed, Chines̶ ̶ ̶hristians were caught in the cross fire of the modernists and the traditionalists: were they simply another superstition? or representatives of a foreign culture? Faced with these suspicions, Christians engaged in what Wing-Hung Lam has called a "strategic theological retreat" (1983:46). Wishing to avoid the divisiveness of denominationalism and the liberal-fundamentalist split, Chinese Christians focused on the imitation of Christ and on character formation. These emphases, which were to become decisive for the later house church movement, were especially prominent in the Chinese Christian leader Wang Ming-dao. Wang believed, on the basis of his reading of Scripture, that Christianity introduced a way of life distinct from anything one's culture offered. The latter, since Adam, existed in a state of continuous corruption (Lam, 77 and Wang, 1981).

Still a tiny minority when the Communists won the civil war in 1949, the Christians faced enormous challenges. Soon the presence of foreign missionaries became an embarrassment and pressure was put on them to leave. The victory of Mao had resulted in an emphasis on Marxist ideology cast in almost biblical images: a putting off the old ways (especially the four olds: old customs, old habits, old culture, and old ideology, and the "undesirable elements") and a beginning of a new life. In 1951 the Chinese government formed the Three Self Patriotic Movement (TSPM) ostensibly as a means of allowing an arena for the freedom of religion, but, many believed, also as a means of exercising government control over Christians.

The challenge provided by this development must be

regarded as one of the most serious to face the modern church. Were Christians to enter this structure and seek to reform or challenge it in the name of Christ? Or did the call of Christ forbid association with a movement some of whose leaders were obviously unbelievers? For leaders like Wang Ming-dao the answer was clear. Having faced a similar challenge during the Second World War, when the Japanese military government demanded membership in a Christian Association, Wang felt this was another challenge to Christian faithfulness. For him there could be no question of joining with these open churches. God constantly places us in situations of difficulty, he wrote, but this is for the purpose of purifying us: "In this situation all that we can do is to maintain thankful and obedient hearts and to endure the inevitable buffeting so that in the end we may become like smooth stones. We shall then be of great potential usefulness for the Lord" (Wang, 1981:-144–45).

Many believers followed Wang's path of refusing to identify with the open TPSM churches, and began meeting secretly in their homes. Ironically during the 1950s any contact with the West was broken off and all open activities ceased so that by the end of the decade there were virtually no open churches. Gradually the TPSM lost influence, and was only reconstituted in 1980 after the reopening of China to the West (Chao, 1988:iii–xxxiv).

During the cultural revolution of the 1960s any known Christian (along with members of the old intelligentsia) were forced into hard labor in the countryside as a means of thought reform. Mao believed a revolution of this kind was necessary every ten years or so to purge society of reactionary elements and maintain a high level of revolutionary fervor. The notorious Red Guard, young members of Communist youth organizations, were left to conduct their reign of terror. Hundreds of thousands died, as they had during the "liberation" of China in the 1940s. But the unintended result of all this was a further spread of the gospel. As one person put it: "The spiritual victories during this period in the modern church history of China were miraculous and numerous, so much so that they continually moved people to song and tears."

The Cultural Revolution took on such a life of its own that often the government itself could not control it, continuing into the early 1970s. In 1976 Mao died and by 1978 Deng Xiaopeng had won power from the so-called Gang of Four, and a new openness swept the country. Churches opened and were soon crowded. But soon after (1980) the TPSM was reorganized, a new period of party control over the state ensued until breezes of openness began to blow again in 1984. Deng has brought a new pragmatism to Chinese politics by putting the practical needs of development over ideology. But as the reaction to the June, 1990 Tiananmen Square incident indicates, the government will set limits to this pragmatic openness to freedom and Western influence.

The challenge provided by the TSPM since its reestablishment in 1980 continues to divide Christians. Many in the West have become enthusiastic supporters of the "open churches," and its leader, Bishop Ding, has become a frequent visitor at Western meetings. These churches are growing and clearly have the support of many believers in China. But these churches are not without problems—informers in the congregation and the close association with the government make many people uneasy. Although many observers feel that the TSPM, in the long run, provides the best arena for Christian ministry, the members of house churches are not convinced. While we do not intend to judge between these views, here we focus our attention on believers in the house churches.

THE DEVELOPMENT OF HOUSE CHURCHES

Whatever the political realities, the amazing fact remains that during this time of persecution and turmoil the numbers of people meeting in small house churches throughout the country has grown, even at conservative estimates, at a phenomenal rate. As we have seen, Wang Ming-dao was one of several Christian leaders who refused any compromise with the TPSM and its sister organization the Chinese Christian Council. Indeed this fact is a major characteristic of the movement we will study. They have conceived of their commitment to Christ as excluding any submission to official regulation of Christian worship and teaching. The political theology that this implies will occupy us later.

Because of the vast rural expanses in China and the prominence given the family in the culture, the meeting of small groups of Christians for prayer and worship has been a characteristic of Christianity from the beginning. In this, of course, they follow a pattern that has been repeated throughout Christian history. But with the government's attempts to register Christians in the early 1950s, the movement received a new impetus. David Adeney lists factors he believes led to the growth of these churches: (1) The breakdown and closure of institutional churches; (2) the deep desire for Christian fellowship during the times of political unrest; (3) the desire to be free of any kind of political control; (4) the new opportunities for evangelism offered by the Cultural Revolution when believers were scattered throughout China; (5) the special work of the Holy Spirit in response to the believers' prayers for healing the sick (perhaps in the light of the absence of regular medical care); and (6) the importance of Christian broadcasting (1985:145–46).

A major characteristic, then, of these groups is their independence from any political control, either on the part of the government or of foreign churches or mission organizations. A further irony of the TSPM churches is that they were established to emphasize the Three Selfs; they were to be self-governing, self-propagating, and self-supporting. While many have questioned whether these characteristics are true of TSPM churches, there is no doubt whatsoever that they are true of the house churches. Indeed when missionaries were forced out of China in the 1950s and churches closed, there were many who felt that there was a real possibility that

Christianity would die out in that great nation. But it was precisely when the Chinese took leadership into their own hands that an explosion of growth occurred.

The question that concerns us in this chapter is: What kind of theological framework has emerged among these house churches?

By examining their own accounts of their experiences we want to discover the elements of their faith that have sustained them through their trials and have drawn so many of their countrymen to Christ. We face several obstacles, however, in seeking an answer to this question. The first relates to how it is possible to generalize over an area so vast and with so many regional differences. This indeed is a serious limitation that should not be underestimated. It is complicated by the unscientific nature of the data available to us, especially that which has been translated into English.

In support of this project I point out that China, while a vast continent, exhibits remarkable cultural unity because of its dominant language and historical traditions. Through much of its history it was ruled by single dynasties. Moreover, as far as I know, all of our narratives come from the majority Han people, rather than from any of the many minority groups (who have their own fascinating stories to tell of the growth of Christianity). Finally, I underline the fact that all the house churches share a common experience of oppression coupled with a relative absence of outside teaching and literature. This has required them to develop a widespread, if informal, network of traveling evangelists and Bible teachers who have facilitated a remarkable exchange among various parts of the country. Of course a more sustained study of house-church theology would have to give more account of the variety within the movement—there are those with a strong Pentecostal orientation, those called the Little Flock or the Born Againers, and so on. But here we focus on the elements all have in common.

But there remains a more serious obstacle to writing about a theological framework of the house church. A common conclusion about Christianity in China in general, and the house churches in particular, is that theological reflection has been virtually non-existent. Lam notes that in the early decades of the century "the weakest area of the Chinese Church was the absence of a rational Christianity that could gain a hearing from secular intellectuals" (1983:25). Douglas Elwood notes that Chinese theology has been almost entirely devotional (or confessional) rather than interpretive, and quotes a leading neo-Confucist scholar, Wing-tsit Chan, as saying: "So long as Christianity fails to come in contact with Chinese intelligentsia, it will have failed to reach the nerve center of the Chinese people" (1975:8–9).

But this objection raises its own questions. To what extent does theology have to be a rational discipline, as it has become in the West? One could argue that the Buddhist and Confucian traditions that the Chinese treasure are not themselves "rational traditions," but rather are traditions of practices and values growing out of paradigm models (preserved in some cases in classic texts). Is it not at least possible for Christianity to develop as a set of practices in a similar way, even if it is based in a unique way, as I will argue, on God's redemptive activity narrated in Scripture? The fact is that churches have grown in China because the Gospel has been perceived to provide what the heart of these people long for; the overflowing of true life.

To argue that the house churches exhibit a theological framework is not to say that further development is not possible or even desirable. Nor is it to say that there will never be a place for professional theologians with university training or a particular body of literature. Special offices and specialized literature may facilitate theological development, but they are not necessarily the only sign of theological reflection—particularly in traditions without a strong written culture. Nevertheless the major evidence for our argument is an examination of the data to which we now turn: What is the symbolic framework by which house-church members understand their faith?

THEOLOGICAL FRAMEWORK
OF THE HOUSE CHURCHES

Living the Life of Christ

The Christo-centric character of earlier theology continues in the house churches. This implies a strong moral identification with Christ that leads to a life of virtue and discipline. Wang Ming-dao echoes many believers when he notes of his country that "the general level of maturity gets lower and lower, what the world needs today is a man of virtue, power and determination who will devote himself to the transformation of the human heart" (1981:49). Following Christ usually means, as we will see, having a strong dependence on the Holy Spirit and the Word of God, but will in any case lead one, Wang continues "to produce the fruits of holiness and piety and to live a life like Christ" (Ibid., 104). The "correct path is not to deviate from life, real life"—a teaching that is thus rooted in real life, says Wang, is truly spiritual (Ibid., 130). Interestingly in this Wang recalls the Confucian teachers in their focus on virtue (jen) as central to the moral life.

But the Christian's focus on morality has a totally different setting than the Confucian teachers; the particular life and sufferings of Jesus. So the life the Christian leads has a particular shape: The Christian has sacrificed all and therefore is willing to suffer for Christ. "For a person to accept baptism means that he/she is willing to die for Christ" (Chao, 1988:58). Another testified that while in prison, the world "died to me and I to the world." After hearing of brothers who died for their faith during a service, a brother began singing two hymns. They went like this:

> The cross was heavy, the pain hard, the way was crooked, but the Lord was present, comforting him in a mild voice "do not worry, I am walking with you." Its meaning was that although the cross was hard to bear and the road is twisted and hard to follow, the Lord Jesus is at your side (Chao, 1988:103).

As Wang Ming-dao put this once, "Some of God's promises are written in invisible ink, only in the flame of suffering do they become visible" (Wang, 1981:71). Another comments: "Every believer must be willing to follow the times (i.e. in which 'freedom of religion' is only a phrase). He must be prepared to sacrifice himself to God. Cadres in any small place can arrest and sentence you without regard for truth" (Chao, 1988:6 of the time of the Cultural Revolution). It may be thought that Christians sometimes pursued suffering as an end in itself, but this is not true. Indeed the evidence is that Christians became very wise in knowing what they could and could not do to avoid arousing the suspicion of the authorities. Suffering was rather an inevitable concomitant, in their particular time and history, of the primary goal: following Christ.

Suffering, then, becomes a key theme in their testimonies and singing, and leads them to strongly identify with the sufferings of Christ. From one testimony: "The sinless son of God paid the highest price on account of our sins, being denied by God. But we are sinners, and we were unclean and full of dross and impurities that needed to be purged before we could be useful to God." When asked to deny Christ, another responded: "The Lord Jesus died for me, I live for the Lord Jesus" (Chao, 1988:40).

Two comments may be made on this theme. Though obviously a prominent biblical theme, this emphasis also reflects the Chinese context—one often overlooked in Western Christianity. It is not simply the fact of suffering that is important but the way its meaning becomes central in their life and worship. It is used, on the one hand, to mark their identification with Christ who also suffered, and, on the other hand, it is used as a typical means of purifying themselves from alternative desires and allegiances—in a uniquely Chinese form of introspection. Accordingly, several agonized while in prison about whether they were truly single-minded in their faith, "Have I really left all for Jesus?" one asked. Thus that suffering is used as a discipline to focus faith on Christ in a way reminiscent of the Buddhist goal of release from desire.

A further comment relates to the exclusivity of this commitment that is interpreted by the house-church Christians as precluding any political involvement. This is not a matter of being conservative or liberal, they insist: It is following God's path. Upon his release from prison in 1980 Wang Ming-dao said: "A preacher should preach only the word of God, and if he mixes his preaching with other things, the preaching will not be pure" (Quoted in Chao, 1988:129). "I know about trends," he noted, "but I do not get involved in politics."

The situated character of their theological framework again becomes clear. It is often concluded that Chinese Christianity has demonstrated a world-denying form of Christian living that is based on a cultural dualism. It is more accurate, according to my reading of the evidence, to say their profound and unhesitating commitment to follow Christ exclusively has provoked the world—as they know it—to attack them unceasingly, and thus, has led them naturally to conclude this world is no friend of God.

Testifying to Jesus

Central to the life and worship of Christians in the house churches is the act of testifying to what Jesus has done. Ordinarily this refers to some particular (often miraculous) intervention or deliverance. When a person has undergone some unusual experience with God that she has narrated often the comment is made: "She has a wonderful testimony." As might be expected, a prominent subject of testimony is suffering, since it is safe to say that all Christians in the movement have experience, either direct or indirect, of suffering—sometimes separation from loved ones, imprisonment, or overt persecution by the authorities. One spoke of his conversion simply as being inwardly transformed into "a deep affection for bearing witness to the Lord."

In the late 1950s it was said: "Now the work of spreading the Gospel on the mainland is being done by those brothers and sisters who have come out of prisons. Their work and testimonies have greatly moved people" (Chao, 1988:6). "There are some brothers and sisters in the prisons who die for God. They have beautiful testimonies for God" (Ibid., 8). When one returned from a time of hard labor in the country, he reported: "My family was exceedingly joyous. I bore testimony to the wonderful things God had done, and we gave thanks, praises, and glory to God."

Giving testimonies, in many ways, is the primary form of evangelism among house churches. After the testimony of a Christian woman who preached to a cadre and healed him it was said: "News of this incident spread far and wide. There was no need to preach the Gospel there" (Chao, 1988:30). Another woman was made to wear a tall "dunce" hat with a board detailing her crime of believing as she was paraded through the village. But this turned out to be simply a form of testifying to her faith in Christ: "It was really an opportunity given by God to give a testimony to bring about the repentance of many and lead them to belief in God" (Ibid., 39).

Services in homes, in fact, are often called "witness meetings." Since there are ordinarily no preachers, and evangelists visit only infrequently, the "sermon" is often nothing but the testimonies of believers (Chao, 1988:116). A report of house churches in the Fujian province reported that "sermons consisted mainly of testimonies and sharing," and in Guangzhou "when Christians came together, they usually shared their personal testimonies" (Ibid., 76–77). In the homes, Christians simply meet to encourage one another with testimonies of what God is doing among them—one is healed, another is released from prison, and so on.

As in the book of Acts, these testimonies have been a powerful means of identifying God's presence. Moreover, the act of giving one's testimony is not simply a report of something that happened, but is itself a part of the way Christians are to live victoriously in the midst of difficult circumstances. To become a Christian is to be brought into the presence of God and to submit completely to him. Thus, when one leader was called to speak at a hastily arranged conference, he realized they did not want him to teach theology, but "to give a message leading the congregation into the presence of God." His own faith he says, is as much "a part of me as flesh and blood and I can never be separated from it. As long as I still have breath left I will firmly believe it." To speak as a Christian is inevitably to testify.

It follows that standing up to give one's testimony in China today is clearly understood to be a political statement of allegiance. To become a Christian is to identify with God's work in a way that necessarily limits one's submission to the state. As one believer testifies: "We will obey the government, but when the government pressures us to deny the existence of God, we are not afraid to sacrifice our jobs, our families, even our lives. We Christians did our jobs, not for mere appearance to please men, but with dedication and singleness of heart as to the Lord." Government authority, then, is bounded by God's rule, which is supreme. One believer, for example, felt his greatest failure was in attempting to escape from prison, rather than waiting for God's timing. Because the power behind the authorities comes from God: "I should submit to it if it is not against my belief and beyond my ability."

Notice that the practice of testimony becomes in itself an expression of theological realities that may remain, for many of them, largely unarticulated. A testimony becomes a central symbol of God's presence and activity in the community. It makes theological, social, and even political statements about their faith. Moreover it plays a central role in that it becomes the means of expressing (and extending to others) the reality of the practical life of virtue and suffering that is the essence of Christian discipleship for believers in China today. While historical and political exigencies—the lack of trained pastors or of Christian literature (even Bibles!)—have given the practice of testimony a special prominence, the role it plays in life and worship expresses deep theological realities that are not visible in any other way. Its importance rests further in the way that symbolically it is linked to other practices that together make up the Christian life among house-church Christians.

Though it is not our purpose to elaborate this here, the central importance of testimony may provide a beginning point for critical theological reflection in the movement. God's reality, though, while it may be evidenced and expressed by our experience with him, should not in any way be limited by that experience. If the relations with the government and thus surrounding culture should change in any drastic way, the role that testimony would play, just as the role of suffering, would be expected to change as well. In that case the same grace and goodness of God would be understood and experienced in different ways.

Prayer

The religious life of Christians in the house churches could be said to consist in equal measure in testimony and in prayer. Just as meetings were often "witness meetings" so they were also "prayer meetings." Here complete dependence upon God was expressed in the simplest way. When something happened, one testified, they would simply close the door and pray. A woman, imprisoned, was once approached by Communist guards because of another particularly difficult female prisoner whom no one could handle. Could she do anything for this person? She began to pray and gradually the other woman began to change; beginning to groom herself and dress normally. When the guards asked what the Christian had done she replied: "I had no strength to change her. I prayed for her, and I believed that God could change her" (Chao, 1988:21).

When a cadre continually bothered the Christians in their meeting, the Christians prayed for deliverance. In one case the woman became paralyzed, in another an animal of the offending official was afflicted, still another became ill. In rural Zhejiang around 1980, it was reported: "Every Christian has a straw mat at home. Whenever they run into any difficulty they kneel down and pray. When the brothers and sisters see each other, they seldom talk about how they are and what has happened and so forth [instead] they kneel down and pray. Thus, the might and miracles of God are frequently seen there" (Chao, 1988:106). In Lincun the meeting place was at one of the sisters' homes: "Every Sunday the Christians would come to this house and everyone would kneel down and pray. After praying they would leave. Why was this? It was because they did not have a preacher, no Bibles or hymnals and the sister herself was not very well educated. So all they could do was pray" (Ibid., 111).

The effects of prayer, as expressed through testimony, were often the primary means of evangelism, as we noted. Many speak of becoming Christians after someone had been prayed for and was healed. Often even non-Christians would come to meetings of prayer. "Through much prayer and concern the Lord listens to our prayers and heals them [the non-Christians] miraculously" (Chao, 1988:61). One group of Christians was even willing to pour themselves out in prayer for the salvation of the entire production brigade to which they belonged. They lived out their prayers by giving help to any who needed it, so that many were moved by it, and almost all of them in fact became believers (Ibid., 65).

Prayer, of course, has always been a prominent element in Christian living, but because of the unique context of the house churches it has come to play a special role in their symbolic system. This was partly a result of the political oppression, for, as someone commented, they felt most free when they were at prayer. Clearly no accusation could be made against them when they met simply to pray (Chao, 1988:68). But the prominence of prayer was also a result of their deep sense of need and powerlessness, humanly speaking. When all other recourse was closed to them, the sense of power offered them by prayer became especially precious. When Christian literature and even Bibles were difficult or impossible to obtain they turned more frequently and emphatically to prayer.

Reading and Study of the Bible

But related to this was the reading and study of the Bible. Always scarce, frequently—especially during the Cultural Revolution—confiscated, and often copied out laboriously by hand, Scripture, even a page or two, was a treasured possession of believers. They believe the Bible is "the complete story of life and death, inspired by God and so absolutely right." One believer undergoing hard labor in the countryside was particularly grateful that "God enabled me to read the Bible and other spiritual books every night."

For house groups, Christian Scripture was understood as containing the way of life associated with following Christ that we described earlier. In his autobiography Wang Ming-dao recounted his experience with Scripture:

> Although I had been reading the Bible regularly for more than six years it was as if all the passages about the way of life had been covered with a sheet of paper. . . . But all of a sudden my heart was opened wide and I grasped the fact that Christ could give eternal life to all who believed in him. In him is life, and it is life he gives to all who trust him (Wang, 1981:69).

Needless to say, for many Christians, the Bible is the only Christian literature they read. As a result, believers read it through many times. And Wang Ming-dao's comments are typical of the attitude of many: "In my preaching and my teaching today the Bible is my only standard. Church traditions and man-made regulations were not my authority," and "[the] beliefs and the message I preached were derived in their entirety from the Bible" (Wang, 1981:84, 111). Sermons, when they existed, were commonly simple expositions of some story or passage of Scripture. One brother when asked to write an article on the "Christian outlook on life" boasted that "the whole article was filled with quotations from the Bible and had very few personal views."

A complete study of the hermeneutics of the house churches is beyond the scope of this survey, but the assumption is clearly present that all Scripture is immediately applicable. As a result, little attention is paid to the original context of passages, and allegorical interpretations abound.

An interesting insight into the informal training programs that have developed, as well as into the role of Scripture, came from one report from North China. There Bible study groups were set up on each night at different locations. Leaders in training visited these groups each night according to a prearranged schedule to lead them in some study. Thus these leaders were learning as they taught. Their goal was to teach the basic doctrines of the Bible as well as to provide messages most needed by the people (Chao, 1988:208).

Clearly, because of the repression Christians have experienced, the symbolic significance of Scripture has been enhanced. Obtaining scarce copies of Scripture has been a powerful means of expressing both commitment to the presence of Christ and solidarity with other believers. The Bible has become even more than usually the concrete symbol of God's presence and power in the community, and the foundation for a way of life that is Christ's life.

Mutual Support of Christian Brothers and Sisters

One of the remarkable aspects of the house church movement is the warm fellowship that has developed among believers and even among groups in various regions. This is especially significant in light of the great variety of mission and church groups that had been present in China before missionaries were forced to leave. In accounts of the church before the Communist takeover, one often comes across references to this or that region being a "Lutheran" or a "Presbyterian" area and so the churches had that particular character. With the rise of the house church movement all this is changed. Certainly there remain regional variations and even doctrinal particularities, but generally people have come to see themselves as Christians. In 1976 one believer commented that various groups do have their doctrinal distinctives, but these "differences no longer alienate them as before.

There is much mutual care among all believers" (Chao, 1988:57). Offerings are "mostly given to Christians in other areas, who are especially poor or suffering from famine" (Ibid., 69).

Accordingly house-church Christians see themselves in real solidarity with believers everywhere. I have heard accounts of Chinese Christians moved to tears when they hear that believers abroad are praying for them. With reference to the support the brothers and sisters provide for one another one testified: "Brotherly love in our Lord Jesus Christ transcends time and space, and no force can block it," and "we as children of God were linked heart to heart, which brought us great comfort"—here alluding to assistance coming from churches overseas. On one occasion when Wang Ming-dao was ill a brother searched the shops to find the mineral water he needed. He succeeded in locating six bottles for Wang! However difficult it was to locate the mineral water, Wang noted, "the genuine love and zeal of that brother are qualities that money can't buy" (Wang, 1981:92).

In an atmosphere of suspicion and mistrust, the freedom and security that comes from knowing you are with brothers and sisters is incalculable. This accounts for the fact that, in spite of the fact that house groups sometimes grow quite large and meet through the night, often their presence goes undetected. In one case a baptism that went throughout one day and into the night was undiscovered despite the concerted efforts of authorities to find out where they were meeting. Little wonder, again, that the political dimension of brotherly and sisterly fellowship leads believers to conclude that they are not to mix with the world—a strong element of Wang Ming-dao's teaching (Chao, 1988:17).

The culmination of this fellowship is awaited in heaven, the believer's eternal home, because, however sweet earthly fellowship is, it is fleeting. But believers in house churches have the joyful confidence that they will meet again in heaven. There, they believe, they will lay down their sufferings to "fly to your true home, where sorrows and tears are no more" (Chao, 1988:52).

CONCLUSION

Clearly we have not discovered all the symbolic elements of the faith of Chinese believers. But these are sufficient to see that this framework is an authentic representation both of their context and of the work of God in their lives. Indeed theological reflection in the sense of a lived framework must be a result of interaction between these elements.

Notice too that all the elements are interrelated. Testimony or prayer, considered by themselves, would give a distorting and indeed unremarkable picture of house-church faith. But put with the central theme of living the life of Christ, and with sisterly fellowship, they begin to paint a full portrait that has proven so amazingly attractive to a people often thought to be fairly resistant to the Gospel.

But as in any situation where the Church is growing rapidly, leaders in China express concern about the rootedness of the new believers. Are they being founded properly on God's Word? Can they withstand the challenges that await them? One might distinguish challenges that are historical and sociological in character from those more properly theological. In the former, one notes that the house church movement has primarily flourished in the countryside. Its members are primarily those without access to educational or economic opportunity. What resources will this people have to face the incredibly complex social and economic issues that face urban China today? Theologically we have already noted the weakness associated with their strong emphasis on experience and Christian living. While this has given their fellowships a vitality and winsomeness that we can only imagine, it has also skewed the reading of Scripture in a particular way. Will the Bible be allowed to speak a prophetic word to these fellowships in the days ahead? Will it allow them to see their Christian obligations in a broader way than they have done previously?

For the present these questions must remain unanswered. Any more complete picture must await reflection by representatives of the house churches as they continue to reflect on the ways of God. Meanwhile, we have much to learn from even a brief encounter with their spiritual reflection.

WORKS CITED

David H. Adeney.
   1985.   *China: Church's Long March.* Ventura: Regal. Singapore: OMF.

Ming-Che Chang.
   n.d.   *Jump Over Mountain Mists and Rapids; The Struggle of My Believing.* Seattle: OMF.

Jonathan Chao, ed.
   1988.   *Wise as Serpents, Harmless as Doves: Christians in China Tell Their Story.* Pasadena: William Carey; Hong Kong: Chinese Church Research Center.

William Dyrness.
   1989.   "A Unique Opportunity: Christianity in the World Today, a Globe Encircling Appraisal." *MARC 14th Mission Handbook.* Monrovia: Missions Advanced Research and Communication Center; Grand Rapids: Zondervan.

Douglas J. Elwood.
   1975.   "Christian Theology in an Asian Setting: The Gospel and Chinese Intellectual Culture." *Southeast Asia Journal of Theology.* 16/2:1–16.

Lam Wing-Hung.
   1983.   *Chinese Theology in Construction.* Pasadena: William Carey.

Wang Ming-dao.
   1981.   *A Stone Made Smooth.* Southampton: Mayflower.

Unpublished testimonies (where unattributed in the text).

Guatemala

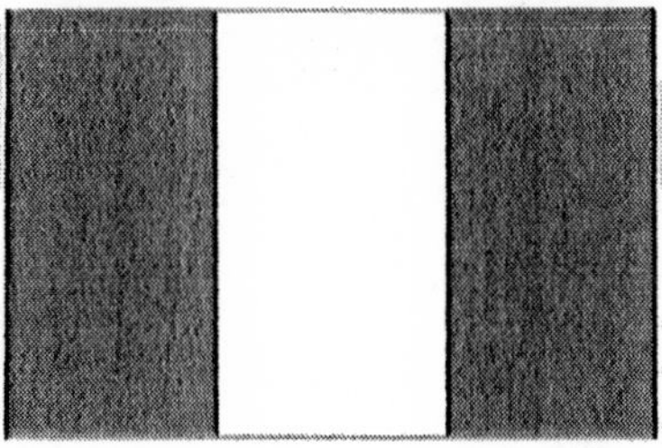

Chapter 3

The Mam Indians of Guatemala

HISTORICAL AND CULTURAL CONTEXT

Guatemala, though invaded by a Spanish expedition in 1523, has perhaps the most vibrant presence of pre-colonial Indian culture of any country in Central America. Nearly half of its 8.3 million people speak one of the thirty Mayan languages. The Mam Indians, second largest of the Mayan groups, are composed of nearly a million people who live in a wide band of the western highlands stretching south from the Mexican border along the Pacific Ocean.

The size of Ohio, Guatemala is sharply divided between the urban elite, living mostly in large, bustling Guatemala City, and the rural poor who survive on subsistence agriculture. Worse, a third of the people, including most of the Indians, must squeeze their living from 2 percent of the arable land, where 70 percent of all usable land is owned by 3 percent of the population. These rural poor grow corn, beans, and squash for food on minuscule family plots of one-third of an acre. If they are fortunate enough to have more land, they grow cash crops of wheat, potatoes, or vegetables. In the fall, after the short growing season, most families travel to the coast—packed together in trucks covered with tarps. There they work as day laborers on vast sugar-cane and cotton plantations owned by foreign multinational companies and a few wealthy Guatemalan families.

This difficult life, which in many respects has not changed for centuries, is complicated for the Indians by the racial discrimination they face daily at the hands of the ladinos, or Spanish-speaking mestizos. To the Maya this Spanish-speaking world is responsible for the ostracism they feel from economic and political power. As one Indian woman explained the situation: "It's unfortunate that we Indians are separated by ethnic barriers, linguistic barriers. It's typical of Guatemala, such a small place, but such huge barriers that there's no dialogue between us" (Menchu, 1984:143). This situation has become especially painful in the last fifteen years as thousands died in the earthquake of 1976 and thousands more in what was euphemistically called *la situación* of the late seventies and the eighties, when the government began waging a savage war against subversive elements. During these years many thousands of persons were eliminated and upward of 100,000 sent into exile in Mexico. Up to the present, people, who in any way threaten the control of the oligarchy or local political hegemony, have continued to disappear, be tortured, or murdered (Scotchmer, 1989:296).

This political crisis has been accompanied by a cultural revolution in which an increasing contact with the outside world, through missionaries, development workers, and consumer goods, has led the Maya to a new search for a viable life. One of the results has been an eager acceptance of Protestant Christianity. In all of Guatemala Protestantism has grown from 4 percent of the population in the sixties to 25 percent (or even 33 percent) today. While the percentage is smaller among the Indians, the growth of the churches is rapid and a third of the Protestants may be Mayan (Scotchmer, 1986:205 and 1989A:10–11).

THE RELIGIOUS BACKGROUND OF THE MAYA

Up until a generation ago it was thought that Mayan religion had, by the last century, been thoroughly assimilated into Catholic forms; existing primarily in a highly syncretistic blend of "Christo-paganism." There is a certain superficial support for this in Indian faith and practice. For example, in one prominent myth Jesus and Mary are chosen to create the productive world (Earle, 1986:168). Moreover, Christian saints figure prominently in the Mayan calendar. But recent study has shown the situation to be more complex—and more provocative—than previously thought. Barbara Tedlock (1983) employing a more phenomenological approach, or reading the religious practices in terms of the meanings the people themselves give, has shown that beneath these surface similarities people have clear notions of the distinctions between these systems and worldviews. At the same time, some anthropologists see common structural elements of a Mayan worldview surviving amidst a great diversity of practices (Reifler Bricker, 1981).

In order to catch a glimpse of the Mam view of the world, then, we must begin with a brief description of the profound interrelation between time and space that is reflected in their everyday life. Their houses are made of straight sticks of cane fastened with agave fibers, covered with adobe. The cane is best cut at full moon—consonant with night and the stable, the earthy and female dimension of life. Doors open to the west, or the south, where they can catch the warm afternoon sun and be protected from wind and rain coming from the east (or northeast). This spatial arrangement—feet east; head west—is the same as the position for the deceased. It reflects their belief of the house being an entity related to the dead ancestors and the earth deity (the moon), in contrast to the active life in the fields—the male domain—ruled by the sun's warmth and vitality (Duncan Earle, 1986:165).

This order is reflected not only in the layout of the space in which they live, but in the temporal ordering of things. Life passes from the rising of the sun, through the activity of the day, to the sleep at night; from the first rains in the spring, through the activity of planting, to the rest after the harvest; and from youth, through the strength of adulthood, to death. Interestingly, the inheritance of the family is fixed at the birth of the first grandson so that the grandparents can divest themselves of their productive (and reproductive) roles, and begin to act as intermediaries between the spiritual world and the earth during their declining years (Earle, 1986:162).

Just as there is an altar in every home, and there are prayers before each day's work, so religious ritual is not a separate part of life, but is integrated into the daily and yearly rhythms. In a sense the Mayan is born with what Duncan Earle calls original debt (rather than original sin) to his or her ancestors and to the earth, which of course are related. The earth (and the ancestors) must be asked for permission before crops are planted, and at the end of the year payment is made to the earth by means of a sacrifice. In many respects, death is the final payment for the enjoyment of life and the use of the earth, as the latter "eats" the person as it might accept an offering (Earle, 1986:163n24).

The pantheon of gods is vague and changing: One, two, three, or many gods may exist all at the same time. "In a sense," Earle reports, "every dialectical interaction between an element and its contextualizing environment may be considered deified" (Earle, 1986:167). In general, prayers reflect a sense of connection with the earth. "Our father," the central deity, seems to have a higher position. Though it is often applied to the sun, it has a floating reference. "The one father is the heart of the sky, namely, the sun [or Kman Kij, 'Our Father Sun']. The sun is the father and our mother is the moon" (Menchu, 1984:13). Before work, men take off their hats and address the sun. At a marriage the couple pray: "Father and Mother, Heart of the Sky, may you give us light, may you give us heat, may you give us hope and punish our enemies—all those who wish to destroy our ancestors. We, poor and humble as we are, will never abandon you" (Ibid.,

67). Kajau, or "Guardian Lord," a lesser god, is identified with the mountains, springs, even with the sky and is felt to be more responsive to the needs of the people.

Under this realm of gods is the Mundo, the layer of productive and fertile earth as well as the place of the ancestors. The lines between these spheres are not fixed, however, for at night, via dreams, the supernatural world can invade the world of the Mayas. Beneath this all is Popol Vuh, the barren place of the devil and San Simon, patron saint of the underworld. This latter often takes visible form as a Ladino who receives offerings at local shrines.

So the Mayan is born into a world that is threatened with suffering and pain. Indeed part of the birth ritual expresses sorrow at bringing a child into such a place. "Suffering is our fate, and the child must be introduced to the sorrows and hardship, he must learn that despite his suffering he will be respectful and live through his pain" (Menchu, 1984:12; cf. her conversation with her father when she saw, whatever her ambitions, she had "no way of achieving them," p. 59).

Yet the goal of religious ritual is a peace and harmony with the spirits, the environment, and with others (Scotchmer, 1989A:17). Among Mam traditionalists this is sometimes called one's *Chwinklal*, the prosperity and security of one's life as measured by good crops and a healthy family. This can only happen as one is made right with the ancestral spirits, mountain deities, and even with the town saints (Ibid., 19), and it is to be shown in the symbolism that permeates the whole of life. The final goal involves nothing less than a reconciliation of all the disorder that exists, through sacrifice, prayer, and shamanistic intervention. And the spatial-temporal metaphysic that underlies these beliefs and practices has shown a remarkable ability to survive incursions from both Catholic and Protestant spiritualities.

Still when the ground shakes and houses fall on loved ones, when the crops do not produce enough for the family, or when the economic hold of the parents is weakened due to smaller and smaller inherited parcels, and people are forced to flee to the city or to El Norte, "we could expect an opening to other ideological options beyond that offered by the local shaman" (Scotchmer, 1986:205).

THE SYMBOLISM OF MAYAN CHRISTIANITY

We have implied that though the structural relationship between space and time has survived to the present, the religious rituals designed to preserve this order have been challenged. The study of religious and social change is a complex affair, but a review of the personal accounts of conversion—our primary sources throughout this study— suggests that there are two major reasons for questioning traditional religion. On the one hand, there are the macro issues of economic and political troubles. Old gods somehow seem less effective against these major world-shaking events. On the other hand, personal issues of illness, and more particularly inter-family strife, drunkenness or unfaithfulness, which too often are not cured by ritual performance, become motivators for change (Scotchmer, 1989A:17–21).

In traditional Mam faith, the ancestors were meant to set a standard for the whole community. Rigoberta Menchu reports: "Nearly everything we do today is based on what our ancestors did. This is the main purpose of our elected leader— to embody all the values handed down from our ancestors" (1984:17). This is what it means for the people to "respect themselves," that is, maintain their identity as people. But when the world is shaken in ways that seem beyond the reach of these "powers" the *religious* tie with them begins to be questioned and people become open to other—Marxist or Christian—ideologies. The vague preordination of traditional religion seems inadequate in the face of major cultural (or personal) crises. Many have found a spiritual home in Protestant or evangelical faith. Among the Mam, the primary denominations are the Central American Mission and the Presbyterian. These together have developed a network of thirty churches and one hundred more congregations, with over 25,000 members, in every Mam municipality of the three western highland provinces (Scotchmer, 1986:206). Becoming a Christian and accepting baptism is a major step, both in separation from the dominant traditional Mayan religion and from the Ladino (Spanish-speaking) Catholicism, and in discovering a new identity as "Evangelicos," or Protestants.

In this context what are the major elements of a Christian and Protestant faith? A survey of the religious symbols that provide models of and for reality will show the essential themes and practices that express and embody their Christian commitment. We will use first-person accounts of conversion provided and studied by David Scotchmer, veteran missionary among the Mam Indians between 1969 and 1982 along with unpublished materials.

THE AUTHORITY OF CHRIST

The primary difference between Protestant and traditional Indians centers on the operative view of deity, expressed both in Kman (Our Father, or Kman Dios, Our Father God), and in Kajaw (Our Lord, or Kajaw Crist, Christ our Lord, Guardian). We have seen that traditional faith affirms a hierarchy of gods, indeed it tends to deify any dialectic relationship between the person and the environment. In stark contrast, for Mayan Protestants, God is the God of good personal relations. He is found nowhere in "things," but he is present without fail in relationships between himself and the believer, or among believers (Scotchmer, 1986:207).

Corollaries of this relate to new attitudes toward the earth and toward other people, especially other believers. Since the relationship with God is immediate and direct— through his son Christ—no other symbolic mediation is allowed. Believers have a keen sense of having direct access to God through prayer and his leading in their lives. While in the army, one Christian testified: "My faith was in the Lord Jesus

Christ. He is the one I trusted in as my helper and my strength every day. Even though I suffered a lot, (but) Christ was with me. Then it was due to God's favor (grace) that he helped me" (PM 131–37). In a time of trial another reported: "I was more in prayer and in trusting God ever asking 'What am I to do and what will happen to me?' I was not thinking that I might get out or not. I was only waiting on God's favor. But God answered my prayer" (Ibid., 355–59).

Worship becomes a matter of inward or personal expressions of praise or prayer to God. The church buildings are barren except for a few flowers placed in recycled milk cans, Altars are missing from homes, replaced perhaps with a Scripture verse on the wall. Participation in worship is a sign of real conversion because of the new relationships with other Christians (which we examine below) and with the "Lord Christ," not because any spiritual power is believed to be mediated exclusively through worship. Indeed, worship can take place anywhere at any time, where these *relationships* with God and others can be enjoyed, celebrated, and renewed. The old spatial and temporal mediation of spiritual power is supplanted (Scotchmer, 1986: 206).

Protestant attitudes toward the earth are affected. Christians feel free to innovate in their methods of farming or in their businesses (Annis, 1987). A believer testifies:

> Another example of my difficulties as a Christian occurred because I began terracing my corn field so that the top soil would not be washed away with the six months of rain. When I began teaching others how to improve their land in this way I felt the anger of my community. Many neighbors accused me of changing what God and our ancestors had given us. According to them we must keep the land just as we received it (MS, 5).

This has to do with faith ("God created the land, the sky, the rain, and the plants to give us life; to all of us and not just some of us"), but it also expresses a freedom from bondage to cycles of nature that the traditional Mayan spirituality reinforces. We will comment further on this below.

But faith in God above all, for the Christian Mayan, is mediated and expressed through relationship with Kajaw Crist, our Lord or Guardian. Sometimes called quite simply God, Christ is felt to be the proximate source of blessing and spiritual power—though all speculation about his nature and relation to the Father is missing. The plethora of local divinities and saints that are acknowledged in traditional Mayan faith, have been supplanted by the single source of saving power, which is Christ. He has been victorious over the powers of evil and can be trusted to save the believer. One Mam leader testifies:

> Kajaw Crist is the one leader for us, a captain, a general who gives wise counsel. He has more authority than that of the people. We essentially are fearful of people with much authority. But Kajaw Crist has greatest power, and much more authority than do these people. That's because God's law (Tyol Dios) is a very sacred authority. More than anything it speaks strongly about our hearts. It speaks about our lives and how they need to be opened, about how we may become stronger believers, who are upright and true in our faith like a soldier of Kajaw Crist. What is it that Dios observes in our behavior? How does Kman Crist look on us? Are we doing what we do with joy? Do we go quickly and do what Kman Crist has told us to do (PM, 461–98).

Notice first that the authority of Christ is related to the law or word of God that is found in the Bible. This plays a very special role in Mam spirituality as we will note. But loyalty to the Bible is tied to a second factor that is clear from this testimony. Following Christ lays particular obligations on believers that cannot be avoided. Here, in continuity with their traditionalist past, emphasis is laid on concrete obedience as a sign of faithfulness. In a survey of Mayan elders, 40 percent from three Presbyteries responded that being saved involved the necessity of works (only 18 percent of the Ladino leaders felt this way). As David Scotchmer explains this, because Kajaw Crist's power to save from evil is total, likewise his authority over our lives is complete (1989:303).

The salvation that Christ brings is in some ways similar to traditional ideas, but in important ways is distinct. Salvation does involve a harmony with others that recalls the quest of traditional faith, though it involves none of the public ritual celebrations and sacrifices. A new Christian says of his conversion: "The changes in my life are many because of this. Most important is that I live and work at peace with my family who also follow the way of Christ" (MS, 2). Belief in Christ, Scotchmer observes, "draws on the cultural truth that the Maya live within a world full of benevolent and malevolent powers" (1989:307).

But there are important differences between Christian and Mayan views of salvation as well. Unlike their traditional counterparts, Scotchmer notes, Mam Christians do not focus on Chwinklal—life's continuity and safety from evil felt in hunger, illness, and accident—but rather on Colbil—that is, salvation as rescue from the threat of sin. This seems to relate to the Protestant dichotomy between spiritual (or relational) religion and the earthly orientation of traditional faith. Their view of faith (did missionary teaching play a role here?) is that it promises a spiritual joy both in this life and the next, whatever the actual physical difficulties that may exist here and now (Scotchmer, 1989:302). In support of such an interpretation, Scotchmer notes that believers are not buried with belongings essential to the journey of the after life as traditional Mayas are. This fits well with the testimony of a Mam leader.

> When I became a Christian, I really believed all my problems would be over, that I would be better off, and that there would be no more serious conflict with others. I have learned that this is not the way it is for believers. Now I know that Satan is able to make us doubt our faith and turn us from following the path that Christ gave us to walk (MS, 2).

Evil in fact has a positive role to play in the life of the believer, as this leader goes on to say:

I am not like many of my Christian brothers and sisters who say that God was punishing me for my sin. Not so, for I believe Christ took all the punishment for my sin on the cross. This evil comes from Satan and the power of sin in others and not from God. But I do believe that God used this to teach me about sin in my own life. . . . I know that I must follow Christ even more closely so that no matter what happens I will walk with him and he will walk with me (MS, 3).

So for Protestant Mayas a single living God is primarily symbolized through Kajaw Crist, the Lord and Guardian, who saves the believer from sin and evil and who responds to her prayer even as he expects complete obedience. Protestant spirituality and the life it represents can be summarized as the Way of Christ, or walking with Christ.

CONVERSION TO CHRIST

What does this do to the traditional interrelationship of space and time in the Mayan worldview? We have seen that traditionally the Mam believe that space, especially the east-west axis is related to the cyclical passage of time, and to the renewal of life, both through the birth of infants and the spring rains symbolic of the renewal of the earth. Sin as seen in this perspective is more of an absence of these blessings of renewal than of any personal or moral shortcoming. Sacrifices, then, are actually subordinated in the mind of the Indian to the universal order that we live in. Prayer and offerings maintain the world rather than challenge or change it in any fundamental way.

For the Evangelico the decisive event becomes the conversion, the point at which the Mam turned her back on the traditional faith and believed in Kajaw Crist. All of life is now reoriented, not to the cycles of nature, but to this great personal divide. Life now has two halves that stand in contrast to each other:

There is nothing better, only God. Well, in my life back then, all I thought about was my money, especially Sundays, not to make purchases [in the market], but to drink with my friends. And depending on what I earned, I spent what I wanted on drink. Not now or ever again will I return [home] drunk. For now in my life, only our Father in heaven has helped me by his love and his teaching given to me. My belief is in our Lord Jesus Christ alone, and for this reason I am happy in the faith because it is the work of God and not of man (testimony in Scotchmer, 1989A:18).

The two halves of life are contrasted in stronger terms than even night and day in the traditional worldview. The line between them, however it is drawn, is irrevocable and unique. The old life often features illness, violence, jail, indebtedness, and often despair; the new one is associated with joy, the guidance of God and his Word, and best of all the promise of eternal life (Scotchmer, 1989A). These changes speak theologically of an even more fundamental transition, from cyclical time, which is viewed in retrospect as a kind of bondage to this world order to a linear or advancing view, in which life becomes a path or way that leads to heaven and to God. In some testimonies this new path in pictured as almost a new order of existence, as in the following:

The gospel! What joy! Only those who are capricious/stubborn reject it! Now I know in my own self that our Father Jesus Christ in heaven is our savior because today on earth there is no one else to save us, only Christ who is in heaven. For only God made the earth and sky, as it says in the word, and gives us "life" (Chwinklal). But now I have really trusted this entirely, for if I do not repent, who will help me. That's the way it is. So now I want to receive more help to be a believer (Quoted in Scotchmer, 1989A:23).

This, of course, has a great impact on Mam attitudes toward the earth, as we noted. It also introduces them to ways of thinking that sociologists have identified with modernization (Berger, et al., 1974). The opportunities and pressures this makes possible belong to a story outside the scope of this study, but which will one day have their own chapter in Mam theological reflection.

GOD'S WORD

One of the most important concrete symbols of the Protestant Mam is the Bible, God's Word (Tyol Dios). From the time of the first Protestant missionary in Guatemala in 1841, there has been a strong emphasis on literacy, education, and the translation of Scripture into local languages. Indeed, the largest missionary organization in the world, Wycliffe Bible Translators, had its beginning in Guatemala and its founder Cameron Townsend figures prominently in the history of Protestantism in Guatemala (Scotchmer, 1986:210–11). It is not surprising then that the Bible, as God's Word, plays a central role in the imagination of the Mam Christian.

Simply to carry a Bible symbolizes one's identity as an Evangelico. Christians universally judge the Bible to have played a key role in their conversion.

> One day. . .a neighbor stopped to visit me and asked if I wanted to buy a New Testament in simple Spanish. I was suspicious, but I bought it because I had nothing to read. This book became very important to me as I read and reread certain parts trying to understand its meaning. Because of this visitor and my reading of the New Testament during some five months, I began to ask him questions and soon became a Christian. The changes in my life are many because of this (MS, 2).

Scripture is a major factor in Christian growth. After becoming a Christian another reports, "I felt God's favor from the word of God and from the hymns when I heard them. I then made every effort to read the word of Our Father God in the Bible, and I became a helper in my congregation" (PM, 32–37).

This last testimony reflects the fact that God's Word is felt most directly in the mind (nabl) and heart (tanmi) of the believer.

> While still a [Catholic] catechist, I began to question the
> mind (nabl) of the priest and many doctrines of the church
> which were not in God's word (Tyol Dios). . . . Because we
> were trying to follow Kajaw Crist "Our Lord Christ" and
> obey Tyol Dios, my brother and I agreed that it would be
> better to resign as catechists than to have them throw us
> out in a big fight. After that we visited the homes of our
> people to say that we were still Catholics but that we
> wanted to obey Kajaw Crist. For two years we met quietly
> in our homes praying and studying Tyol Dios (Quoted in
> Scotchmer, 1989A:21).

Little wonder that Scripture and texts of Scripture are
primary symbols in Mam Christianity. Bible society posters
and Scripture texts decorate the walls of churches and homes.
Homes and churches in fact are often identified as belonging
to Evangelicos simply by the presence of Dios te Ama (God
loves you) or a similar text scribbled at the home's entrance.
In worship the Bible plays a central role. Worshippers are all
expected to share in the reading and discussion of the text—
even if it is read haltingly by a child or semiliterate adult, or
perhaps recited by memory.

> When we enter into worship, this moment should be used
> eagerly to hear the word of our Father God and we should
> think about it eagerly. When worship is over we should
> have a clear idea and hopefully a bit of advice for ourselves.
> Because this moment is a time for us to nourish ourselves
> Spiritually. But not just this; rather we are to put into use
> what we have heard and do it eagerly (PM, 523–33).

During 216 worship services monitored, the New Testament was cited 72 percent of the time, half of these coming
from the Gospels (with Matthew being the overwhelming
favorite). Major emphasis in the teaching was on the God of
creation who meets our needs, and the ability of Christ to
forgive sin and give power over illness, demons, and conflict in
relationships (Scotchmer, 1989:298–99).

Though carrying and reciting (or posting) Scripture becomes itself a symbolic act charged with spiritual significance,

Tyol Dios has none of the mysterious totemic significance present in objects used in traditional ritual. It is rather the way the actual spiritual knowledge and authority of Christ is mediated to Christians. And the believer's mind and heart receive benefit from this Word. It "is read, studied, memorized, cited, explained and applied as God's Word to God's people" (Scotchmer, 1989:289–99).

The emphasis on Scripture and reading has had a major impact on the lives and values of Indians. Converts regularly refer to the importance of reading, literacy, and education in their lives. One, looking back on the period of his conversion, notes that most people thought school and reading was not for the Indian. "An Indian is supposed to work with his hands and his back. Most of my family and friends said that only those who do no work but just sit and read or write need to go to school. Although I didn't realize it at the time, I now believe that learning to read and write has been the greatest change for me" (MS, 2). Another comments on God's ability to give understanding:

> The mind (wisdom) that God gives us is a knowledge of very great authority in order that we might be able to provide an explanation that is clearer for our brothers as well as an explanation that is softer (easier to understand) in order that they might know more about the faith in Our Lord. With this in mind and for this reason I am working in the church. . . . They chose me to work in a program for the production of literature in Spanish, in order that I work with literature production as well as sell books, like the New Testament or other similar material with God's word in it (PM, 420–33).

The full effects of this on Indian culture clearly have yet to be worked out. But like peasant peoples in other parts of the world, the Mayan Indians are experiencing a fundamental transformation from an oral culture, with its traditional authorities rooted in the ancestors, to a literate culture, where authorities become written texts. For Protestants and many Catholics this authority is found supremely in the Scriptures.

SISTERS AND BROTHERS IN CHRIST

A final symbol that we examine is that of the new relationship Christians enjoy in the church of Christ: Sister, brother (*hermana/o*). One of the primary ways Christianity is worked out among the Indians is in the new identity Christians assume. Clearly this is one of the most important and sensitive gauges of cultural change. Rigoberta Menchu, a Quiche woman active in the movement for Indian rights, speaks often of the control and mutual support provided by the community. The eyes of the community are on us, she notes. We have freedom, but within that freedom we must "respect ourselves," that is, maintain our traditional identity (1984:49). On one occasion when soldiers came to take their land, "the women asked [one of them] how he could have become a soldier, an enemy of his own race, his own people, the Indian race. Our ancestors never set bad examples like that" (Ibid., 138). In the light of this, the new distinguishing characteristic takes on great significance. Mam Christians learn to think of themselves not only as Indian, but as brothers and sisters, *hermanos(as)* in Christ. Indeed, their sense of being Indian, while not lost, is qualified by this new relationship. And historic patterns of discrimination, while not overcome altogether, "must bend to new rules and expectations for how brothers and sisters relate within the church" (Scotchmer, 1989:303).

David Scotchmer reports that the terms sister and brother are universally used and recognized as the distinguishing characteristic of Guatemalan Protestants. When complete strangers are introduced as *hermanas in Cristo*, they express a unity that transcends social status and ethnic origin. Becoming a Christian of course does not mean effacing their Indian identity. For example, very seldom does a Mayan woman make a decision to follow Christ without her husband (or she does so at great risk of persecution, even divorce). Religious loyalty continues to be initiated and maintained by the male household head, with the wife making her decision after

observing the real changes in her husband. But once committed to Christ's path the new converts are expected to abandon
their former ways and associates and identify with other
believers by faithful attendance at church. Within a year or
two, believer's baptism will signal full membership in the
church (Scotchmer, 1989A:23–24).

Traditional kinship and community ties are being se-
verely challenged and eroded in Guatemala today. With the
decline of the father's ability to sustain his family, or to pass
viable plots of land to his sons, goes the corrosion of his
authority in the family (Scotchmer in personal correspond-
ence). Religion, like the economic system, becomes more
individualized as the struggle to survive becomes more
intense. Protestants are somewhat better off than their
Catholic counterparts—largely because they escape the heavy
costs associated with the annual religious festivals, but they
are still largely landless (Annis, 1987).

For people who migrate to the coast to work (as high as 70
percent in some Indian churches), or flee to Mexico or the
United States, the church, the brothers and sisters, becomes a
new extended family vital often to their economic as well as
to their spiritual survival. This new identity virtually replaces
that of the traditional patron saint or religious brotherhood
(Scotchmer, 1989:304). It is expressed through the free organization of the local churches, the choice of their own leaders
and the mutual recognition of responsibility for one another.
It is hard to overemphasize the importance of this arena of
freedom for people who, in many cases, have not had any
meaningful control over their lives for centuries, and as
Scotchmer points out, enjoy virtually no voice in national
politics.

This final practice expresses what we have observed
throughout this study that, for Mayan Christians, faith is
expressed primarily through relationships rather than ritual
acts. Indeed the practice of relating to fellow believers takes
on itself overtones of ritual—the greetings, kisses, and
salutation in letters and sermons. These touches that often

seem to gringos (North Americans) simply an excess of piety are essential expressions of their new identity.

Nor is this new relationship restricted or reserved in any sense for an in-group. Two important factors reflect a universal intent in these relations. First, an awareness of God as creator of all people has led believers to an awareness of his universal Fatherhood over all people. Listen to this testimony:

> When I first read God's word, I did not understand it as I do now. Before I only heard that part of God's word that talked to me and my needs. Now I see that God loves all of my community, my race, my nation. I now see that God especially loves the poor, the stranger, the widow, the orphan, the sick, the hungry, and the prisoner. God does not reject the poor as people do. God created the land, the sky, the rain, and the plants to give us life; to all of us and not just some of us. We have been given God's image but this image cannot be what God wants if we work in vain, if we are hungry and sick, if we are threatened and killed. If we are made in his image, how can this be like God? (MS, 5).

A second indication of the broader reference of this new identity is found in the major thrust of Christian work, as seen through the eyes of Mam believers. Scotchmer sums up all that is required of a Christian in terms of building up God's kingdom, the church. "The final goal is the incorporation of men and women into the true family of God so that all may be considered brothers and sisters" (1986:211). So a Mam, identifying himself or herself as a *hermano* or *hermana* is portraying a new, personal center of gravity applicable to all people, rather than a new exclusive identity. While not effacing their context as Mam Indians, it clearly puts this within a new and larger perspective, where belonging can perhaps shed an even more vibrant light than it had when constrained by the limitation of birth, village, language, and social status.

SUMMARY: THE BEGINNINGS OF A CRITICAL THEOLOGY

These then comprise some of the symbols of a Mam local theology. They must be seen, however, as parts of a whole way of life that is known as Evangelico. As Clifford Geertz points out, they find their meaning in the texture of everyday life that they produce rather than any system that ties them together. Believers now faithfully read the Bible (and affix it to their homes and churches), they embrace each other as brothers and sisters, and seek diligently to follow the path of Christ. At the same time, they no longer sacrifice to the mountain deities, or make pilgrimage to the shrines of saints of the village. They studiously avoid the town fiestas, and they do not drink the local beer or dance to the marimbas. They must avoid feuding or unfaithfulness. All of this is part of the new path they follow.

But then are they any longer Mam Indians at all? Do not the things they avoid make up the essence of this culture? Yes and no. True, they must give up some of what has been made of this culture, but this is, in the Christians' minds, not what is best in that culture. After all, that culture has said that God must be worshipped and obeyed, that the very crops depend on such obedience. The culture also says that Mam live in a world of spiritual presences, powers that must be acknowledged and managed. Finally, the traditions say that people living together must care for and nurture each other. To all of these values, the Christian Gospel, as Mam believers have understood it, says "yes." In fact, the testimony we have heard gives us some evidence that these values are not only preserved but enhanced, albeit in a different form. They are featured in such a way, that, from our North American point of view, we see something about the Gospel (and perhaps about our own culture) that we did not understand before.

In other words, the Gospel that is taking shape in Mam culture has already begun to demonstrate the critical dimension of theological reflection. The practices of the Christian faith have met and challenged the entrenched practices of Mam culture. David Scotchmer recounts one of the most striking illustrations of this from the history of the Synod of the Presbyterian Church of Guatemala in 1981. There an Indian delegate told about outside ladino landowners insisting that the Indians abandon their long-held communal lands. After he finished his story, one by one, Indians from other Presbyteries came forward to tell similar stories, until, at the end, all the Indians stood facing the remaining ladino delegates and a few missionaries. Scotchmer comments: This event "raised the issue of brother/sisterhood to a level previously unknown in a church dominated by Ladino leadership where Indians could perhaps be seen, but not heard" (1989:306). Would the issue be resolved along the ethnic lines the society dictated? Or, would a higher standard be invoked?

After much discussion—often heated—and eager prayer, a commission was delegated to deal with the dispute. It was discovered that the outsiders claims were false and in spite of reprisals, and even the disappearance of some Indian leaders, authorities at the highest level were confronted. After a long struggle the Indians eventually won the right to continue using their communal lands (Scotchmer, 1989:306). Though the theological reality was the new, higher level of relationships in the body of Christ, the results were seen in the bright light of social and political realities. Most importantly the process, though not without its pain and disappointment, developed from the integrity of the peoples' faith itself. Theology was developing a critical dimension.

WORKS CITED

Sheldon Annis.
> 1987. *God and Production in a Guatemalan Town.* Austin: University of Texas.

Peter Berger, Brigitte Berger, and Hansfried Kellner.
> 1984. *The Homeless Mind: Modernization and Consciousness.* Hammondsworth: Penguin.

Duncan Earle.
> 1986. "The Metaphor of the Day in Quiche: Notes on the Nature of Everyday Life." In *Symbol and Meaning Beyond the Closed Community: Essays in Mesoamerican Ideas.* Ed. Gary H. Gossen. Albany: State University of New York.

Rigoberta Menchu.
> 1984. *I, Rigoberta Menchu: An Indian Woman in Guatemala.* Ed. Elisabeth Burgos-Debray. London: Verso Editions.

Victoria Reifler Bricker.
> 1981. *The Indian Christ, The Indian King: The Historical Substrate of Maya Myth and Ritual.* Austin: University of Texas.

David Scotchmer.
> 1986. "Convergence of the Gods: Comparing Traditional Maya and Christian Maya Cosmologies." In *Symbol and Meaning Beyond the Closed Community: Essays in Mesoamerican Ideas.* Ed. Gary H. Gossen. Albany: State University of New York.

———. Appended testimony of Mam believer is listed in text as PM (Protestant Maya).

———.
> 1989. "Symbols of Salvation: A Local Mayan Protestant Theology." *Missiology.* 17/3, (July): 293–310.

———.
> 1989A. "Life of the Heart: A Maya Protestant Spirituality." In *World Spirituality: An Encyclopedia of Religious Quest* (New York: Crossroad).

Barbara Tedlock.
  1983.   "A Phenomenological Approach to Religious Change in
           Highland Guatemala." In *Heritage of Conquest: Thirty
           Years Later*. Edited by Carl Kendall, John Hawkins, and
           Kaurel Bossen. Albuquerque: Univ. of New Mexico.
Unpublished testimony (MS).

Philippines

Chapter 4

A Catholic Folk Theology of Manila's Squatters

THE SETTING OF CATHOLIC CHRISTIANITY IN MANILA

Unique among the nations of Asia, the Philippines has over four centuries of Christian presence. Almost 90 percent of the more than fifty million people claim some allegiance to Christianity—most are Roman Catholics, Protestant missions being largely a twentieth-century phenomenon. The popular religion that has resulted is often blended with elements of traditional faiths. But the continuing vitality of this popular Catholicism and its community-shaping power make it worthy of careful study by students of local theology. As with the Mam of Central America, we do better to see this popular faith, whatever the influences that have shaped it, as having an integrity of its own.

We focus here on Manila, the teeming primate city of the Philippines. Most of the forty-plus language groups of this Malayo-Polynesian people are represented in the city, though we will focus on the values of those groups—largely Tagalog speaking—called "lowland Filipino" (Hollnsteiner in Lynch and de Guzman, 1973). It should be remembered that this is our meaning when we speak in this chapter of "Filipino Culture." A city of only 220,000 in 1903, Manila grew, by 1960, to more than one million people, over half of whom were born outside the city. By 1970 the population was 1.3 million (3.2 million in the greater-Manila area), a figure that had doubled by 1990 and will double again by the turn of the century—to more than 12 million in metropolitan Manila. (Hollnsteiner, 1976:174).

While the earlier segmentation of the city had been ethnic, since World War II when 80 percent of the city was destroyed, divisions have become largely economic. The rich and the small middle class have progressively moved out, leaving the inner city to the poor, who, on some estimates, make up 80 percent of the core population. Of these one-third are squatters—that is people who build their houses on any available land—vacant lots, empty spaces along river banks, and even on the vast garbage dump that stretches along Manila Bay. This last group has recently attracted the attention of anthropologists and missionaries, as forcing in a particularly poignant way the problems of social change and modernization.

Benigno Beltran, a priest who has worked with this rapidly growing population for years, estimates that there are three-thousand families who live as scavengers on the garbage dump in the section of Manila called Tondo. Smoke rises perpetually from the fires on the dump and hangs over the area, which has come to be known as Smokey Mountain. There, families live in makeshift huts collecting bits of plastic or bottles to sell in order to eke out a living. Beltran, a priest of the Society of the Divine Word, in his years of working with these people found them to possess a profound and almost unshakable faith in God and his provision, even though the teaching they had received, when it existed, had been deficient. Along the lines we have been following in this book,

Beltran wondered: What do these people really believe about God and Christ?

During the early 1980s Beltran began interviewing people about their beliefs and comparing the results with previous surveys of folk beliefs in the Philippines and elsewhere. This led him to a major study based on a carefully selected sample of some five thousand persons. His purposes were to (1) determine the extent to which the Christian message is known and understood, so that (2) problems could be identified for a more effective communication of the "Christian symbolic universe" (Beltran, 1987:30). In order to achieve a uniformity of results interviews were conducted orally (in Tagalog) and allowed for only yes or no answers. The limitations of this method he recognizes, but argues that they are compensated for by the breadth of coverage and the controls on the data, which he notes allows for a 95 percent level of confidence and a 0.05 margin of error (Ibid., 42).

This sociological survey differs to a great extent from the participant-observer method we have been using throughout our study. Interestingly, the occasional intrusion of pictures and stories into Beltran's study offers illumination that his data is unable to provide. But the study is an extremely important one and will repay our careful examination in this context. We apply the same methodological questions to his data that we have to the narratives we considered elsewhere: What are the beliefs and practices that structure the symbolic world of their Christian faith? How does this hold together? And, how does it reflect (or reject) the dominant values of the Filipino worldview? To prepare for this last question we turn first to a brief survey of these cultural and religious values.

LOWLAND FILIPINO CULTURAL VALUES

In spite of influences from over four centuries of colonial history Philippine society has developed a unique set of cultural values. It is largely a bayanihan (sharing) society that stresses "tradition, authority, personalism, family ties, inter-dependence and harmony rather than innovation, autonomy and achievement" (Espiritu, et al., 1976:67). Thus, the Filipino tends to have a visual imagination that views life holistically and personally. As a result, Beltran notes, religious symbols and images tend not to be cognitive landmarks so much as "evocative objects [that] arouse religious sentiments, shape values and attitudes and guide behavior" (1987:127). It follows that we can expect less precision and clarity in expressions of faith than we might encounter in groups more verbal and cognitive in orientation.

But the dominant characteristic of the Filipino people is their underlying commitment to personal and social values. Filipinos see themselves as persons in relation in which the self flows into other selves. Social scientists have long noticed this fundamental orientation of "getting along together," what earlier was called "smooth interpersonal relations" (Lynch and de Guzman, eds, 1973). These values were seen to revolve around the concept of hiya (or shame, a deep-seated respect for decorum and the desire to preserve it), which was often defined negatively in terms of a weak ego (Bulatao, 1964 and Espiritu, et al., 1976:65–77).

Recently this approach has been radically recast in a positive light, with the concept of kapwa (fellow being or shared self) in the center. Virgilio Enriquez feels it is very important to expand the previous notion of getting along (pakikisama) as a motivation for behavior, to the idea of a shared humanity (pakikipagkapwa) as a fundamental orientation (Enriquez, 1989:31–34). This relates the Filipino social orientation to their fundamental dignity (karangalan) rather than to the more surface conception of shame, which leads to simple adjustment to others for the sake of harmony. In the "Philippines' value system Kapwa is at the very foundation of human values" (Ibid., 36).

Building on this understanding, Enriquez analyzed eight levels of interaction with outsiders, which moves from mere civility and adjustment to outsiders, through a development of mutual trust, toward the level of fusion or (pakikiisa) oneness (1989:31). The dynamic and changing face of these levels of interaction clearly constitutes the driving force of Filipino culture. The question we ask is: How will theological understanding reflect this orientation?

(2)   A second major value is the awareness and acceptance of evil. Beltran comments: "The empathy with suffering and death, sometimes bordering on a gruesome fascination, is a part of everyday life in the Philippines. Funerals in the village are not complete unless the coffin is opened before interment and pictures taken of the deceased, together with all the relatives" (1987:138). Filipino movies and literature reflect this same fascination with abuse, humiliation, and violent death. And the acceptance of a world in which these things are common has given them a strong sense of fate, and the so-called wheel of fate, as being major factors in a person's life.

A prevailing attitude toward life, then, is one of resignation—ganyan lang ang buhay (that is the way life is) is a common expression. For the Christian the question arises: Does this orientation simply translate into a sense that God will take care of us, replacing fate in a functional sense, or must Christian's rage and struggle against the surrounding evil? One senses that Beltran struggles with this question as he analyzes the results of his surveys. He writes:

> Every time I go up Smokey Mountain, praying for serenity, while anger and frustration rage within, I look down on the scavengers' hovels, blurred and annihilated of all color by the smoke from burning pieces of rubble and bone and plastic—and I see another garbage dump of decaying emotions. . . . Yet, as I rage against the dying of the light, the scavengers themselves can laugh so easily. They sing the songs at Mass with broken voices, but with little trace of my own rancor or grief at their misery (1987:176).

Related to this is a sense of the times through which life passes. The seasons of life are recurrent, but they flow in a linear way from birth to death. This time can be good or bad, but one cannot stop the flow. The goal then must be to fit into it, to harmonize with its contour. Things will happen in their right (fulfilled) time, so one had better make the best of it.

One would be mistaken, however, to conclude that this desire for harmony reflects a lack of energy or vitality. To the contrary this is a people with enormous energy and creativity. Many of those in this study—rising while it is still dark to begin their daily round of activities, display enormous ingenuity in finding ways to scrape together the money and food they need to survive. Mary Hollnsteiner has called this cluster of values a personal need-power framework. That is for the Filipino the stress "in her culture goes to need and power rather than order" (1976:179–80). She helpfully goes on to describe the Filipino horro vacui in both space and time; they tend to fill the space around them with the permutations of their social interactions (a fulfillment reflected in the intricate carvings in their churches, or the folk paintings on their jeepneys). [7]

Here, then, is a people for whom relationships, and social interactions of all kinds, reflect a fundamental human desire for fellow beings. These values permeate the whole of their lives even to the preparation and consumption of food and to the structure and furnishing of their homes. Before we look at the implications of this for their understanding of Christianity, we turn to a brief survey of their traditional religious understandings, insofar as these are understood.

FILIPINO RELIGIOUS VALUES

In the beginning, according to the Filipino myth of origin, the first man and woman emerged simultaneously from separate sections of a bamboo. The man exclaimed "ba" (whence babae, the Tagalog word for woman); the woman "la" (whence lalake, or man). Looking around they together exclaimed "ha" (hence Bathala, or god) (Beltran, 1987:160). Further myths speak of original conditions that Bathala placed on the man and woman, which, when they broke these conditions, led to all kinds of natural and personal evil—a story like many others from around the world (Dyrness, 1990:45).

Bathala, the high god lived alone in the sky. He was believed to have human characteristics, but being exalted and distant no one could talk to him. So Bathala created "anitos" to be intermediaries, between himself and the people. Since the anitos are closer to the human world they are more concerned with human needs, and therefore sacrifices are appropriately offered to them. In early Filipino history these beings were thought to reside in sacred groves or caves.

This is the spiritual universe of the Filipino, peopled as it is with many spirits, called anitos, and a high god who is remote and inaccessible. Meanwhile, subject to the many vicissitudes of life, the Filipino feels vulnerable to evil and in constant need of protection. Amulets and images are often assumed to have magical power. Food is left for the dead in cemeteries—especially on All Saints' Day—and sacrifices are offered to avoid crop failure. "Filipinos see reality as seamless. One thinks nothing of laying hands over a goat, or of divining from tawas the cause of one's sickness, or of attributing to kulam or spirits certain mental and psychological signs of discomposure" (Maggay, 1991:15).

This religious temperament, altered as it is with various amounts of education and the omnipresent influence of Western culture, persists among those who identify themselves as Catholic Christians, resulting in what has come to be called "Folk Catholicism." This unique blend of practice and belief includes, Frank Lynch believes, peninsular Spanish and Mexican additives and the preexistent Malay base we have briefly described. Though there may be relatively little understanding of official church teaching or much familiarity with the hierarchy, the people exhibit a remarkable frequency of attendance at Mass, accord a high place to trust in God, and engage in intense social practices associated with various feast days of the church calendar (Frank Lynch, in Hollnsteiner, 1979:123–30).

Whatever our final assessment of this kind of faith, the mission of Father Beltran fits well with the purposes of our study. We can appropriately ask: For people of such a popular faith who are struggling to survive in Manila's giant garbage dump, what is the meaning of our confession that Jesus is the Christ? To put it in terms we have laid out for ourselves, what is the symbolic universe of this form of Christianity? To discover the answer to these questions, Father Beltran carefully prepared and tested a survey that would gauge the participants' understanding of Christ and Christianity: "Can one only learn the whole truth through Christ? Should we be ashamed to call Christ God?" A company of carefully trained seminarians conduced the survey of over five thousand persons in the mid 1980s. The results, which we analyze here, appear in his important book *The Christology of the Inarticulate* (1987), which is a major contribution to reflection on how people "do theology."

SOME BASIC SYMBOLS OF FILIPINO FOLK CATHOLICISM

Hesus Nazareno (Jesus the Nazarene)

In the large downtown church called Quiapo Church there is an image of a black Christ, the work of some unknown Mexican artist that was brought to the Philippines in the sixteenth or seventeenth century. The image, dressed in purple and wearing a crown of thorns, is down on one knee and carries the cross on its shoulder. In the survey, this image of the Black Nazarene was chosen by the highest percentage (32.9 percent) as the image they felt closest to. Beltran tells the story of his father, who is one of the many devotees of the image.

> When my father, who was an intelligence officer in the army, was captured in 1941 during the war against the Japanese, he was tortured along with his companions in

Fort Santiago [in downtown Manila]. He was told to dig his own grave and when he bowed, anticipating the blow of the Japanese executioner's samurai sword, he prayed to the Nazarene. With a shout, the executioner brought down the sword a hair's breadth away from my father's scalp. My father attributed his reprieve to the intervention of the Nazarene. Since that time, he has been a passionate devotee of the Hesus Nazareno and never fails to attend the novena in honor of the Nazarene whenever he comes to Manila (1987:116–17).

This story is one of the countless stories of those who have appealed to the Nazarene for help. There is always a long line of people waiting to see the image. When they approach they touch the image, or rub it with a piece of cloth, which they will take home to rub on someone who is ill.

On the feast day of the Nazarene, January 9, the image is carried through the streets of the city, amidst throngs of rowdy and ecstatic people who crowd around in order to touch the image. Many of the men from the squatter areas who follow perform a particular ritual on that day. They all wear white T-shirts, and rolled up jeans, they wear no shoes and each wraps a towel around his neck. This prepares them to make a vow that they promise to perform in honor of the Nazarene during the coming year.

In some ways this image plays a role much like images play in popular religions around the world. But for the Filipino particular dynamics are at work. First, it seems that images provide a particularly dramatic witness to the incarnation of God in Christ. This image is, Beltran believes, a "witness to the incarnation, to the reality of God's presence and to our participation in the very life of God" (1987:130). Remember we have noticed that the Filipino feels an excruciating vulnerability to the evils of the world, and only a very concrete fellow feeling can offset this cosmic sense of weakness. Images tend to give the believer a sense of confidence, almost an invincibility when the rituals are performed faithfully and properly.

Note, in the second place, that performance of the rituals

associated with the Nazarene are essentially social. Filipinos, *rituals*
we have seen, are most themselves when united in some
common action—to join with others in such a procession
appears to satisfy a deep need of pakikipagkapwa (being in
relation), both to God and to other people. Frank Lynch
comments on this: "I suggest that the image represents for the
persons honoring it a means of bridging what at times seems
to be an immense gap or distance between the saint [in this
case Jesus] and themselves" (Lynch in Hollnsteiner, 1979:129).

But, thirdly, there is a more properly theological motive
at work in their identification with the image. While, we have
seen, God is perceived as remote and therefore uncaring, the
Nazarene expresses in very concrete form the pity God feels
for his people. In many ways the most characteristic attribute
of God for the Filipino is this mercy or pity (the Tagalog "awa"
has both connotations), especially in his ability to intervene
on behalf of a people in extremes. Beltran comments: "The life
of the Nazarene is the all-seeing love and compassion of God
operating under the conditions of temporality" (1987:234). So,
that homage to the Nazarene is a way, for people with little or
no human solace or material security, to recognize and hold
on to the reality of God's redeeming love as they are able to
understand it.

Jesus on the Cross

Related to this is the ever present image of Jesus on the
cross, which is found in hundreds of forms among the
squatters. This was the favorite image of 23.2 percent of those
surveyed, but 74 percent believed that the greatest gift of Jesus
was his death on the cross for our salvation (Beltran,
1987:122). In one form or another, images of Jesus on the cross
adorn their modest homes, their jeepneys, their clothes, even
the karitons they use to collect their bottles and paper. Its
presence marks an important dimension of their faith.

In one sense, of course, the emphasis on the passion or
suffering of Jesus is characteristic of Catholic Christianity,
which in turn is heir to the development of medieval mystical

piety. There, preoccupation with the sufferings of Christ grew along with the explosion of penitential practices, but also with a deepened understanding of Christ's own humanity (see John Bossy's description of this traditional Christianity, 1985). But, in a more immediate sense, this image of Christ relates to the language of sacrifice that is so much a part of Filipino culture. In traditional rural religion the sacrificial killing of pigs or chickens was common. But even for an urban and literate people, as we have noted, the awareness of suffering and vulnerability is a poignant part of their daily lives.

Somehow these people understand that God is wrathful and loving at the same time. So, in the survey 91.7 percent believed the death and resurrection of Christ is the "reuniting of human beings to God" (Beltran, 1987:99). Clearly the precise understanding of this is not clear, or rather, its connotation shifts according to the context. On one level Beltran believes "the sight of their crucified God increases the resolve to survive" (Ibid., 123). It is not simply God's example, but the motive that led to his suffering that carries meaning. For the self-sacrifice of Christ is the most visible and accessible image of God's mercy. It shows that he is a God that can be appealed to when one has no other recourse.

Beltran goes on to note that this motive and this example stimulates a change in the people as well. "Their sympathy for the sufferings of Jesus inspired the masses to recognize the sinfulness of their 'loob' (inner self). . . ." (1987:140). But just at this point the particular weakness of Beltran's method becomes apparent, for here we long to hear the people talk about these images in their own words. What situations in particular call attention to this image of Christ? Are these images placed around because of a mere superstitious faith that God will protect them when he sees his Son? Does the image cause them to think about their sin and, if it does, what does this sinfulness mean to them? These questions remain unanswered, though we return to some of them in the conclusion.

Self-Flagellation

Various rites of self-flagellation have been common in the Philippines for generations, and they are found among this group of squatters as well. In fact, these acts of penance were practiced by an amazing 36.3 percent of the respondents. During Holy Week people resolve to go barefoot, or to lash themselves with broken pieces of glass embedded in wood, or to whip themselves with rope and bamboo sticks. They even bring these implements of penance to the priests to be blessed! (Beltran, 1987:114–15).

Perhaps they do not see this as atonement so much as a more general identification with the suffering of Jesus, which plays such a large role in the Filipino imagination. In any case the penitents—mostly male—testify to an overwhelming sense of joy and peace, and many say they feel no pain or that the wounds heal instantly when they bathe in the sea after the flagellation. Again, traditional and cultural values blend to produce a grass-roots asceticism that is deeply embedded in the religious symbol system of the Filipino.

Again we would like to be more specific: How do their own sufferings relate to those of Jesus? In what ways are they unlike Jesus' suffering? But these are questions we cannot answer—indeed the people probably do not know themselves. What they do know is that their precarious lives incline them to find in the victim-Christ a refuge from the fearful prospects of life. And for many, actively seeking to share his suffering makes more real the identification with him, and, hopefully, allows the supplicant to enjoy the boundless mercy-pity of the father.

Santo Niño

A further image important to Filipino piety is the Santo Niño—27.4 percent preferred this as the image closest to them. Like the Nazareno, this image of the Holy Child has a long history in the Hispanic history of the Philippines. The first such image was supposed to have been given in fact by

Magellan to Queen Juana of Cebu at her baptism in 1521. Later in 1565 when Cesar Legaspi besieged Cebu and his soldiers set fire to the village, the image was found unburned in a house that was being looted (Beltran, 1987:118).

No other image arouses such feverish devotion in Manila today. On the third Sunday in January it is borne on a fluvial parade accompanied by crowds of dancing children, who afterward enjoy a shower of cookies and native oranges. Recently, various forms of the Santo Niño have appeared as an army officer or as a revolutionary. Certainly whatever their understanding of the theology behind it, this is an image of incarnation in which God enters and shares their world.

Again, this is an image with deep resonance in Filipino culture, where children are revered and where innocence is treasured. Clearly the ritual celebration of this image— through the fiesta in January or the care of the image at home—intuitively counteracts the keen awareness of evil and vulnerability that is so much a part of their experience. Is there a parallel with the involvement in suffering? As I can actively share in Jesus' suffering and its benefits, so I can share his innocence. As with the suffering, however, the precise nature of this innocence and the means of sharing in it, are probably only imperfectly understood.

Pasiyon

Perhaps the most powerful expression of Filipino folk Catholicism is what is called the pasiyon (or the reading of the passion story). During Holy Week groups gather to read or recite the entire passion narrative, a reading that is interrupted only for opportunities to eat together and socialize. Apparently the history of the practice, unique to the Philippines, has its antecedents in the custom of reciting long local epics. The early missionaries took advantage of this custom, replacing the epics with the gospel narratives (Lynch in Hollnsteiner, 1979:127).

The event is a chant rather than an oratorio, that is, it does not move toward a climax. In fact when they reach the end of the story they do not stop, they simply start over again at the beginning. But notice that the practice is a communal one, all who want may join in the reading of the story. So the reading brings the people together around this central narrative of Christ's suffering and death.

One might argue, as Beltran does, that this practice serves to set the living community of Filipinos within a larger story as they join voices in the singing, they join with Christians from other times and places, and, most importantly, with God himself. It is, Beltran believes, "a mirror of the collective consciousness of the Filipino masses" (1987:186). They sing, in other words, not "primarily for the sake of singing but to come to terms with God and increase communal feeling" (Ibid., 264). In fact, Beltran believes that the oral patterning of the pasiyon reflects the high value the Filipino places on harmony and interiorization (Ibid., 213).

It might be asked how far Filipinos identify with the pasiyon as being historical, as Beltran implies. Is it reflective of their historico-salvific orientation, or perhaps more of their mystical and communal orientation? Perhaps he is right in seeing their identification with history and with salvation as an inner, personal one rather than an outward, objective understanding. But is it sometimes the case that the mystical identification actually impedes any objective reference?

CONCLUSION

As our questions have implied, this local theology is the most difficult one to properly understand and evaluate. Not only are the cultural values very different from those in the West, but the ritual and symbolic world is Catholic rather than Protestant, as in our other case studies. The Protestant observer traditionally has been tempted to see these practices as carryovers from their pagan past rather than resulting from the impact of the Christian Gospel. If this is the case, these Filipinos do not need theological development, as we have been arguing throughout this book, but rather a conversion from idolatry to faith in Christ. When my wife and I were young missionaries new to Manila, one of our closest friends was a priest assigned to this area of Tondo. In one conversation we spoke at length of what it meant to call people Christian. At one point I admitted somewhat sheepishly that most of my fellow missionaries were fairly certain that these people needed to be converted, and we had spent most of our time working to that end. The priest's next remark surprised me: "You go right ahead," he said, "evangelism is the most important work we all have to do."

While a part of me still agrees with this analysis of things, there are elements of the people's faith that I cannot dismiss so easily. What do we make of their day-to-day dependence on God? How do we account for the central role that Christ's death plays in their imagination, however imperfect their understanding of that event? And most importantly, what do we make of their deep-seated sense of vulnerability to all the evil in the world, and their correspondingly deep hunger for God to save them? A recent study found that the poor in Manila tended to clearly perceive God as all powerful, while rich people mostly thought of God as nurturing (Maggay, 1991:15). Clearly these are realities with great theological significance. We would do well, then, to continue our practice of studying them descriptively as expressions of a real religious system, and then ask how a critical theology may begin in this context.

We begin by reminding ourselves of the visual and communal nature of the Filipino imagination that gives their faith—in Beltran's words—a thaumaturgical thrust. Whatever the abuses to which images, processions, and fiestas are subject, it is inconceivable that a genuine faith, at home in Filipino culture, would not find expression in such visible and social forms. In some sense, faith in God, repentance, and worship would always be public and social events, whatever their inner reality. In fact, if we were to search for some paradigm practice that captures in some central way Filipino cultural values, the procession and fiesta would come close to filling that role.

But what is the felt religious need that is met by such events? Beltran suggests that the problem Filipinos feel most deeply is the need for "expiation of personal guilt not the propitiation of a wrathful deity" (1987:177). This follows from their keen sense of being personally vulnerable, of having what used to be called a weak ego. Sin, then, has to do with some personal failure, having missed the mark, whether by actual mistake or mere finitude. It leaves them feeling exposed, liable to suffering, afraid.

Celebrating the pasiyon, or honoring the Nazarene, then, becomes a way of expiating this sense of guilt by realizing and expressing an actual solidarity—a being together with others and with God. Even the flagellants express a kind of solidarity in suffering with others and with God.

Images, for their part, become a sign of God's presence and concern. Beltran comments occasionally that no one mistakes the images for God (or a god), but rather they see them as signs of God's presence. This reflects their very concrete and visual imagination, and ought not simply be critiqued in terms of Western abstract ways of thinking. Again, however subject to abuse, the concrete presence of symbols of God's presence would seem to be a necessary means of maintaining faith for the Filipino.

For people whose religious imagination has been shaped almost entirely by texts and abstract ideas—wherein theology has been defined in terms of loci, or categorical classification—the centrality of processions and images is problematic. The visual and symbolic dimension of faith and worship in this Western tradition is always secondary and illustrative. The substantive points are abstract, the stories illustrate and suggest application of these central issues. For the Filipino imagination the issues appear to be reversed—the dramatic and visual are of the essence; abstract and dogmatic concerns would seem to be peripheral. As Beltran admits: "The connection between Trinitarian teaching and the daily life of moral endeavor, community, and worship from which ideally the doctrine should live is often very tenuous" (1987:238).

But this way of experiencing the world has clear resources that the evangelist and teacher ought to be able to exploit. Christ seemed to focus his teaching in paradigm stories and enactments of grace, which we have learned to call signs; he seemed always reluctant to summarize his teaching in ways the rabbis (or later, Western theologians) would expect. Two particular examples may be given with respect to the Filipino situation. First, can the high value placed on "fellow feeling" be used to express the reality of God's relation within the Godhead and our relationships within the body of Christ? These realities, when seen from our analytic and atomistic way of thinking, have been among the most difficult for Western theology to grasp. "If humanity and relatedness are directly proportional," Beltran notes, "then the fundamental responsibility is to give oneself away as perfectly as possible; the fundamental human right is the right to do so" (1987:245). This, he goes on to argue, is really the heart of the doctrine of the Trinity. At least, we might add, this is one important dimension of that teaching, a dimension often missing or inadequately understood in our Western individualistic contexts.

A second example might be ways in which our understanding of Christ may be approached in this context. In traditional teaching, we explain Christ's person and work in terms of categories of thought: What is the relation between his deity and his humanity? Or, what is the nature of the Incarnation? The practices that we have examined suggest that an alternative approach might be in terms of our mystical and communal experience of God's presence, as symbolized by our participation in a procession or event. The image would then be a sign of God's merciful presence; it would serve to highlight various dimensions of the reality of Christ in a single experience.

There are obvious limitations here: How is the experience identified as of God in particular, and not a more general human or social experience? Here the limitation we noted in the introduction becomes evident: How is our understanding of a symbolic system adequate to express the reality and presence of God? Beltran recognizes this weakness. It is not enough, he admits, to speak of mere social or economic alienation. "The deepest source of alienation transcends social and economic structures. Only God can save us. One of the most important focus [sic] for theological effort in the Philippines would then to be the confrontation of the fact of sin, of evil, of brokenness and despair, of having missed our destiny, with the process of God's self-giving" (1987:179).

While there is much discussion in Beltran's study of the relation between these practices and Catholic teaching, very little time is spent asking how these might be confronted with the stories and images of Scripture. In a careful study of pakikisama (harmonious relationships), for example, Evelyn Miranda-Feliciano points out that Jesus, and even more so John the Baptist, did not fit in with the group from which they came. Their lives pointed to a different kind of solidarity. "Our 'pakikisama' must somehow 'light up' others as well," she points out. "So by our words and deeds, our companions are led toward constructive, meaningful lives" (1990:26).

Beltran admits his findings show areas of concern. Only 2.5 percent of the respondents chose the image of Christ as King as being their favorite image. What does this indicate about the nature of religious authority, or the way moral decisions are made? Here a whole series of biblical imagery—from the word of God at creation, to Christ's cleansing the temple and Christ as King of Kings and Lord of Lords in John's revelation—confronts and perhaps corrects a heavy emphasis on God's mercy and pity.

Happily those involved in teaching in this context are picking up precisely at this point. In a recent study prepared for parish instruction in the Philippines, one of the leading Catholic theologians, Carlos Abesamis, uses as a central component the idea of God's reign-kingdom. From an understanding of this—as illustrated by the Beatitudes—he goes on to develop the ideas of Good News, deliverance for the captives, and even the resurrection of the dead. Interestingly, Abesamis makes generous use of Jesus' parables to illustrate the character and the demand of this reign of God that appeared in Christ.

If this notion of God's reign, made visible and real in Jesus' life and death, can be connected with the images and symbols that are part of the religious heritage of this people, a powerful presentation of the gospel may be possible. But the possibility exists that this might mean more than simply a theological development, as it has meant in our other case studies. It might result in something that looks much more like a revolution. One has the feeling that Beltran and Abesamis would agree. Certainly evangelical leaders are thinking along these lines. One of the most articulate, Melba Maggay concluded a recent study of problems of communicating the Gospel in the Philippines in this way: "The strong cognitive ethos of Protestantism needs to be softened by a feeling for the romance of ritual and intuitive ways of expressing faith. . . . The task of evangelism must be sensitive to the longing for access, for traffic with the supernatural forces that govern most Filipinos' lives" (1991:21).

WORKS CITED

Carlos H. Abesamis.
    1988.   "A Third Look at Jesus: A Catechetical Guidebook for Bible Facilitators." Quezon City, Philippines: Claretian.

Benigno P. Beltran.
    1987.   *The Christology of the Inarticulate: An Inquiry into the Filipino Understanding of Jesus the Christ.* Manila: Divine Word.

John Bossy.
    1985.   *Christianity in the West: 1400–1700.* Oxford: Oxford University.

Jaime Bulatao.
    1964.   "Hiya." *Philippine Studies* 12.

William Dyrness.
    1990.   *Learning About Theology From the Third World.* Grand Rapids: Zondervan.

Virgilio G. Enriquez.
    1989.   *Indigenous Psychology and National Consciousness.* Tokyo: Institute for the Study of Languages and Cultures of Asia and Africa.

Socorro Espiritu, Mary R. Hollnsteiner, Chesster L. Hunt, Luis Q. Lacar, and Lourdes R. Quisumbing.
    1976.   *Sociology in the New Philippine Setting.* Manila: Alemar.

Mary R. Hollnsteiner.
    1976.   "Urbanization of Metro Manila." In *Changing Southeast Asian Cities.* Eds. Y. M. Yeung, C. P. Lo, and Frank Lynch. Oxford: Oxford University.

Frank Lynch.
    1979.   "Folk Catholicism in the Philippines." In *Society Culture and the Filipino.* Ed. Mary R. Hollnsteiner. Quezon City: Institute of Philippine Culture.

Frank Lynch and Alfonso de Guzman II, eds.
    1973.   *Four Readings in Filipino Values.* Quezon City: Ateneo de Manila University Press.

Melba P. Maggay.
    1991.   "The Indigenous Religious Consciousness: Some Impli-
           cations for Mission." *Patmos.* 7/1.
Evelyn Miranda-Feliciano.
    1990.   *Filipino Values and Our Christian Faith.* Manila:
           OMF.

Kenya

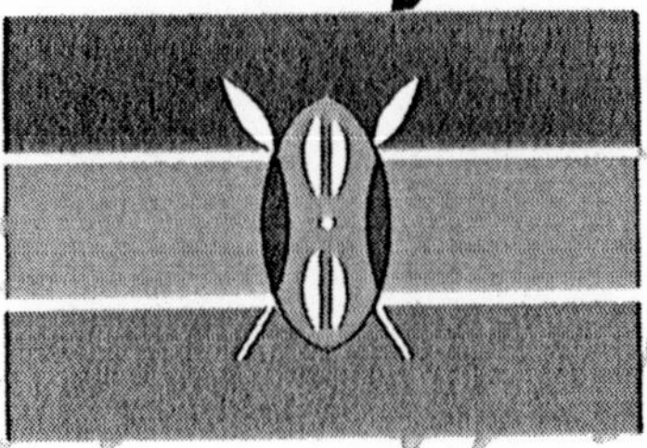

Chapter 5

An Akamba Local Theology

THE AKAMBA PEOPLE OF KENYA

Comprising the fourth largest ethnic group in Kenya, East Africa, the Kamba have for centuries occupied the plains that stretch eastward from Nairobi. The Machakos and Kitui districts, an area about the size of the state of Maryland, are home to almost two million Kamba. (See Amin and Moll, 60–62 for the background material we discuss here.)

The history of the Akamba people is unclear. They probably represent a northward migration of Bantu people from the Kilimanjaro area or a westward drift from the coast. In any case, about four centuries ago they settled around Mbooni, where, taking advantage of the rainfall and fertility, they came to depend on agriculture rather than on the traditional hunting—though the Kamba are still known as skilled trackers and fearless elephant hunters.

In the nineteenth century they became prosperous by trading ivory with people on the coast. But the future was not to deal kindly with the Kamba people, as one of their own prophets prophesied. Masaku, a famous diviner and medicine man (for whom, by corruption, Machakos is named), predicted the coming of the railway—the long snake—and the Europeans who would divide the country. Masaku left the region in disgust when his place, later Machakos, became a thriving administrative center. His fears were not unfounded. Imported rinderpest soon decimated the Kamba herds and the railroad resulted in a ban on expansion into vacant lands. Famines became common. But the deeper crisis was a cultural and spiritual one. Perhaps because they more readily cooperated with the British colonial rule, the Kamba's own cultural institutions were challenged. While, as we will note, traditional authority was exercised by the elders in family and clan meetings, the British appointed "chiefs" who became common. But this was an essentially alien political order, and, as in many places in Africa, its deleterious effects are still being felt.

The Kamba are skilled craftspeople and their products—woodcarving, woven baskets, bracelets, and necklaces made of iron and copper—have fueled a major handicraft industry. But unlike their Kikuyu neighbors, initially they were slow to adapt to modern agricultural methods, preferring instead to serve the colonial regime in the King's rifles or work on foreign farms. Poor agricultural methods and deforestation due to charcoal production (mostly for sale to those in big cities) have resulted in declining productivity and desiccation of the land. While the Akamba have more recently reached a higher level of agricultural productivity—and indeed around Machakos produce some of the best coffee in the country—still the challenge being mounted to their social order and the continuing economic struggle, even periodic famine, have become the inevitable context for their thinking about God.

CULTURAL AND RELIGIOUS VALUES

According to an Akamba myth, Mulungu (or God) put the first Kamba man and woman onto Mount Nzaui where they were joined by another couple from the middle of the earth.

Mulungu sent rain and the land became fertile. The Akamba prospered. They were originally created to live forever, and God sent a chameleon to tell them this news. But the animal lingered on the way and stammered while delivering the news. Suddenly the swift weaver bird interrupted him and announced they would die and disappear like the roots of the aloe tree. Then, the myth continues, they began to die (Amin and Moll, 1983, and Gehman, 1985:133).

Death, life based on a fragile fertility, and the family—these are the major themes of a worldview in which sacred and secular dimensions are inextricably bound together. Perhaps fundamental to this is what Gehman calls the cosmological balance, or equilibrium one seeks for in life (1985:114–20). But lest this be understood in a static way, life for the African in general, and especially for the Kamba is one of constant fluidity and transition. Reality is marked by a trajectory that begins with birth, moves through circumcision (or initiation into adulthood), to marriage, death, and finally ancestorship. These stages provide the cohesiveness that binds together all aspects of existence (see the excellent description of this in Sofola, 1979). But notice that one seeks to facilitate this process, to celebrate it and adapt to it. One does not attempt to transform it in any fundamental way.

The social unit that underlies this order is the family and the clan—each possessing its own totem. The political authority lies with the elders, who are always sought out for advice, which is often couched in long and flowery speeches. One finds one's identity and indeed one's place in the order of things within this context. Marriage (including a bride wealth of up to one hundred goats), naming, and initiation ceremonies are all meant to solidify one's place in the order and thus become ways promoting the flow of life.

John Mbiti (1971) has used a description of Kikamba tenses to illustrate this flow of reality. Since Kikamba has no single word for a clear and definite future—though it has several words for various senses of the past—Mbiti believes that time for the Kamba flows into the past. The trajectory goes from the present to the past with relatively little sense of a specific future.

Circumcision ceremonies have traditionally been important (and often problematic from a Christian point of view) because of their perceived role in this trajectory of life. Both males and females take part in two different initiatory experiences—a shorter one at age four or five, and a second, longer one at puberty (Amin and Moll, 1983:60). These experiences not only mark entrance into adulthood, but more importantly they become the means of passing down the traditions, the order, of the tribe—they, too, relate more to the past than to the future. Under the impact of modernization this rite of passage is no longer as important as it once was, but it still provides for Christians an opportunity to think about Akamba attitudes toward the trajectory of life and the role that Christian sacraments might play in the time of a person's life.

Much of the cultural, even the religious order comes to focus on the earth and its fertility, or its harmony. Nature is, in its ordinary state, harsh and even cruel, it is not necessarily something beautiful. Sometimes the rains come and the crops grow. Sometimes it is dry and the people go hungry. Again the purpose of work, even of religious ceremonies, is to facilitate, as far as possible, the order; to promote the trajectory of things.

The religious dimension of life is everywhere evident—indeed it is hard to separate out the realm of faith from all the other parts of their lives. For the Akamba, religion has a role to play at every point because the spirits and their influence are important everywhere. John Mbiti, who is himself a Kamba, notes "There is no place and occasion when African peoples may not perform acts of worship or of reaching into the spirit realm, through sacrifices, prayers or invocations" (1971:93). The spirit world is very real and surrounds and penetrates this world in a very tangible way (Gehman, 1985:59 and Mbiti 1971:133).

It is hard to overemphasize the importance of this

interconnection of worlds for the Akamba. The Western conception of a secular world distinct from the spiritual (and personal) world is unthinkable for the Kamba. Stanley Mutunga, who helped with these interviews, has underlined the holistic worldview that is reflected among Akamba Christians. Since there is no split between the human world and the world of spirits, there is no distinction between a sacred and a secular time. All times and places have a spiritual dimension to them; Wednesday is just as much a holy day as is Sunday. Of course there are nominal Christians (and non-Christians) among the Akamba, but even these will have a view of life and the world in which spiritual powers and realities are central— a fact with obvious implications for evangelism and apologetics.

The major component of this other world is the spirits of departed ancestors or the aimu—the primary objects of attention in ceremonies and sacrifices. Ordinarily they are seen as intermediaries or channels of the power that properly belongs to God. The spirits are dangerous, but with care, they can be approached and manipulated. When misfortune of some kind strikes, one must seek to discover the cause—often by calling in the herbalist or diviner, and, by proper ceremonial intervention, correct the problem.

Offerings are usually accompanied by some kind of invocation. Libations, for example, may be poured out and accompanied with these words: "We give you, the community of our grandfathers, this little amount of beer, so that you may drink it with us" (Mbiti, 1971:92). There are ceremonies of blessing in which an elder person, spitting lightly, says: "May God go with you," and there are purification rites that are used to counteract a broken taboo or ceremonial impurity by applying a concoction of various herbs and the contents of a goat's stomach.

The key figure in the disposition of power in the community is the mundu mue, or the diviner. This person is the most closely related to the ancestors and therefore one of the most highly respected members in the community. This testimony of a mundu mue, collected by Richard Gehman, gives some sense of the diviner's power in the community:

> My mystical power is not from anywhere but from God. It is not surprising that when I was born, my parents and the midwife witnessed that I had a beard, two bright teeth and my hands were holding two round balls, as hard as stone. . . . The two balls indicated that my mystical powers will be for the betterment of my fellow Akamba to keep them from the disturbance of witches. . . .

> The spirits of my great grandfather claimed me from the family for this duty. They taught me concerning the ways of healing men and women who have been affected by [spirits]. My medicine is really brought during the night through visions and the direction of the aimu. I am told to go to such and such place and I will be shown something to collect or do there. I go to such places at any time I am told by the aimu. When I need a new revelation concerning a new sickness or even what would happen among my people, it is a requirement to drum and perform a rite so that the mystical beings may come, dine and advise me concerning the future and teach me how to play my mystical tool to help the people affected (1985:87–88).

One might say that the goal of religion is putting the community of people and nature into proper working order. It has, in other words, a functional character. African religion, John Mbiti has argued is "utilitarian, not purely spiritual, it is practical not mystical" (1969:67). God is utilized rather than worshipped. The spirits are manipulated rather than simply honored.

Because the goal is to bring the ancestors and God into the dynamic present of human life, and indeed extend this present by marriage and offspring and the proper management of the natural order, religion comes to focus on the present. It is as if the demands of this order, this human community, were so strong that they absorbed all the attention of even that other world.

Death, then, plays a much more positive role in this worldview than it does, say, in North America, because it is the way in which one moves from this dynamic present into the world of the spirits and takes up one's place of influence in that spiritual dimension. There, ancestors continue to exercise their authority. The rituals of death intend to preserve the memory of the departed ancestors, as a means of strengthening the community.

As in other case studies, Western education and economic development have had their influence on this way of life. But in many ways, people, especially in the rural areas that all Africans look to as "home," still live out this way of life. We ask then: What are the implications of this view of life and religion for those who have become disciples of Jesus Christ?

NOTES TOWARD AN AKAMBA THEOLOGY

Although there were missionaries earlier—the first came to East Africa in the mid-nineteenth century—it was really the East African revival in the 1930s and 1940s that gave impetus to the rapid growth of the church in East Africa. Already in the 1960s, John Mbiti reports that fully a third of the Kamba, who probably numbered then about a million, were Christians. Most were members of the Africa Inland Church, which was founded by missionaries of the Africa Inland Mission (Mbiti, 1971:5–20). The number of Christians has at least doubled by now, as Kenya boasts that 75 percent of its population is Christian (see the tables in Mbiti, 1986).

An important window into the world of Akamba theology is embodied in the life and writings of John Mbiti. Mbiti has come to be known as one of the most articulate and influential African theologians. He was raised in an Akamba family who were active in the Africa Inland Church (AIC), and he early became an active Christian. In the late 1950s he studied in Britain, finishing a Ph.D. at Cambridge in 1963. His dissertation, published in 1971 under the title *New Testament*

Eschatology in An African Background, remains a pioneering attempt to rethink Christian theology—in African categories.

While Mbiti expresses appreciation for his background, the work contains an explicit polemic against what he sees as a narrow and literalistic interpretation of theology. That he was not encouraged by AIC leadership in his graduate studies seems clear not only from his critique of the missionaries' teaching, but also from his subsequent career in the ecumenical movement, with which the AIC has had no relation. Professor Mbiti currently lives and works in Switzerland.

While we will follow our pattern of using narratives of Christians, these will be used in this case against the backdrop of Mbiti's study and in relation to popular hymns used in AIC worship. As elsewhere, theological themes will be placed in relation to the practices that have grown up in the churches.

Salvation as Deliverance From Evil Powers

The major emphasis on a local Akamba theology would clearly be on salvation as deliverance from evil powers. Akamba religion, as we have seen, focuses on the management of power relations in the community and between the community and the spiritual world.

In a typical case, a women was subject to nightly visitations that kept her awake. She was told these were godly visits and eventually she would become a witch doctor. An evangelist came to her village and, she later testified, "he explained to me who Jesus was and that he could deliver me from 'those satanic attacks.' Although at first I was skeptical about his interpretation of my experiences, I felt it was time to try any remedy that would save me from the otherwise apparently deadly bouts."

Another believer testified that "after my spiritual transformation. . .a dramatic change began to occur in my life. One area in which even my critical parents pointed out with astonishment was obedience. Prior to salvation, I was notoriously a disobedient boy. . . . But thank God I am now a changed man." It is interesting that the power called for has to do with deliverance from the spirits' influence, but it also is needed to bring peace within the community. As the first women testified: "The verse that says 'forgive them for they know not what they are doing' has had a lasting impact in my Christian life. I have learnt this, over the years through my interaction with my extended family members."

Accepting Christ as Savior

The transformation that takes place at salvation is always associated with the power and work of Christ. In fact, there is a recurring reference to accepting Christ as Savior. "The following Sunday we attended the nearby AIC worship center at Mbiuni and publicly accepted Christ as our Savior." And "knowing that my life was not right with God, I accepted Christ, for the first time as my Lord and Savior." Thus, the event of accepting Jesus is often equated with salvation. One woman lamented that though she was a moral person raised in a Christian home, "I had not yet come to a personal relationship with the Lord." She describes the event of becoming a Christian as boldly stepping forward "to invite the Lord into my heart."

Baptism

Salvation leads to the high importance given to baptism as the second naming ceremony in which Christians are given a new name. Mbiti comments: "It is the most impressive rite of the new religion and culture. From the very start of a full-scale evangelization, it was administered in the 1950s by missionaries" (1971:110). He goes on to quote the reminiscences of older believers who remember the first public baptism. It was an "impressive sight as Brother Hurlburt led these men into the water and baptized them. The banks were crowded with men, women and children" (Ibid.).

Since family and kin groupings are central to Akamba culture, this incorporation into a new family immediately became important. The communal character of faith is emphasized along with its familylike atmosphere. This latter is symbolized by the common practice of calling fellow Christians brother and sister. Even growing up in a Christian home did not automatically make one a Christian, as the testimonies reiterated. One women admitted she taught Sunday School for years, but when an evangelist got through to her she realized that "in spite of my good morals and deeds both at school and home, I was not really a child of God. I boldly stepped forward to invite the Lord into my heart."

Keeping One's Testimony

The public and decisive character of conversion leads to a particular theology of the Christian life. This is referred to as keeping one's testimony. One woman, who consulted with her husband before she acted on the evangelist's advice ("since," she said, "I could not make such a major decision on my own"), spoke about their conversion. "From what we had seen others do, I warned [my husband] that we should be serious with our decision. That is, after we accept the Lord, there should be no afterthoughts about going back to 'our vomit.'"

Another believer, who spoke of being a changed man, described the Christian life in these terms: "I also testified about my spiritual birth at my home church. The Lord has helped me to keep my testimony since then." He went on to say that he had lost many friends, but that "I cannot sacrifice my testimony in order to keep compromising friends."

This way of following Jesus as it is sometimes put, refers to living a life of purity, but even more deeply it has to do with remaining true to the original commitment to Christ. Temptations are pictured in the form of inclinations to go back to the former way of life; to dependence on the spirits. One woman spoke of a major testing during the illness of a son.

According to our traditional belief, I was supposed to take him to a local herbalist for treatment. However, knowing that the herbalist will enlist satanic help, I decided not to take him but just pray. My husband could not see anything wrong with taking the dying baby to the herbalist even though we were now Christians. His mother became furious (to say the least). But I held to my belief that the Lord whom I had accepted was able to heal the child. This was the first major miracle that the Lord performed. The child got well through my prayers.

As one follows Jesus in this decisive way, the witness is unmistakable to those around. The woman quoted above goes on to say: "This became not only a lesson to me but an opportunity for others in our large family to see the power of God and consider accepting the new religion."

Often this testimony takes the form of an active witness to others about Jesus. Christians in Kenya and among the Akamba feel a great need to tell others about Jesus. Thus, mission trips and subsequent sharing times in churches and Bible schools become a common feature of Christian living— a continuing influence perhaps of the East African revival.

A further dimension of this commitment to Christ was the keen expectation of his return to earth at the end of the age. John Mbiti's major criticism of the theology the Akamba had developed was that their unwavering focus on a literal, future return of Christ led to a false spirituality. This had, in his view, two consequences. First, it focused too narrowly on certain teachings of Scripture, while neglecting others. For example, it tended to overlook some of the biblical teaching about earthly justice. But secondly, as a result of this narrow focus, it tended to place so much value on heaven and the future life that it did not give proper value to life on earth.

We have seen some evidence for this in the reaction against moralism and a focus on personal acceptance of Christ. But is it not possible that this emphasis on Christ's return is not because the missionaries imported a false spirituality from abroad, but rather because it expresses something significant about the African context? This may be true in two ways. First, the importance given this anticipation may result from the momentous change in the center of gravity of the Akamba worldview from the past to the future.

Now events are not collecting in the past, but building toward the future. So far from belittling work in this world, this expectation may put our earthly projects in a better, and more hopeful, light.

Secondly, waiting for Christ's return may relate to the centrality given Christ in the battle with the spirits. The fact is that traditional religion throughout sub-Saharan Africa places a great emphasis on life as being a spiritual battle between the powers. Deliverance from evil powers will of necessity become a key theme of any local theology that responds to the issues of this context. Even Mbiti admits that many of the African Independent Churches (not to be confused with the African Inland Churches of the Akamba) have developed a parallel stress on the delivering activity of the Holy Spirit (1971:56). Is it not possible that the keen anticipation of Christ's return relates to this deep-seated longing to be finally freed from the evil influence of the powers? We will see further evidence for this when we consider the hope Akamba have for life in heaven.

View of Ministry

This leads Akamba Christians to develop a particular view of ministry that is worth noting. As in the traditional religions of Africa, while the reality of religion permeates everyday life, the specialized ministries that promote the flow of power are central to the life of the community. We have seen hints that designation, whether by birth or special endowment, as a diviner is an extremely important part of the social order. Similarly, for Christians among the Akamba, ministry has the rather special sense of activity within the church that furthers the cause of Christ and the manifestation of his power.

Almost without exception, testimonies make reference to ministry in this specialized sense. After conversion, one points out that he was able to "keep his testimony" and goes right on to say: "I have since been appointed as Sunday School teacher in [a particular AIC]." Another testified how the Lord had taught her to rely on him for everything.

> He also opened doors for me to do ministry at our local church. I was doing things I would never have imagined I could ever do. I was leading several adult prayer meetings, [I was] choir director, Sunday school teacher, and above all, I organized prayer meetings for girls who had completed schooling like me. This had never been tried in our church and it really gave me a big challenge but also a rare opportunity to minister to them.

This is the woman who had come, at her conversion, to see that the "good morals" of her parents were not enough to make her Christian. All this activity ought not to be confused with a kind of works necessary for salvation. It is rather a sign of the importance placed on ministry within the church as a means of displaying and promoting the power of the Lord Christ.

To have a husband or children in ministry likewise becomes an important goal of Christian living. As one woman testifies "I thank God because all my children are now Christians and one of them is a very successful pastor with the AIC." If life is lived in a struggle between powers, and God is the Creator and Lord of the spirits, Christians must give themselves to the work of furthering the Lordship of Christ, and ministry is the favored place for activities of this kind.

Lively Hope in the Bliss of Heaven

One finds some further evidence for Mbiti's criticism in a final theme of Akamba local theology that we examine: In testimony, and, above all, in songs and prayers, the Akamba find deep consolation in a lively hope in the bliss of heaven. Of course, Christians everywhere wait for the blessed hope of the appearing of Christ to set up his kingdom. But this became such an important theme of their Christian thinking that Mbiti made it the central theme of his dissertation.

While, as we pointed out above, Kikamba does not have a

future verb tense that points to a concrete future event, Akamba Christians have developed a lively sense of the future that focuses on the return of Christ. Mbiti argues that this is an imported idea from missionary theology. Gehman believes it is more a reflection of clear biblical teaching. In any case it has become a hallmark not only of Akamba theology, but of the African church generally.

Like the context around them, life after death is sometimes portrayed in a materialistic way. But it always focuses on the concrete, bodily return of the Lord. Hymn 20 in the Kikamba hymnal:

> Jesus Christ is coming again.
> To take us up above to our home;
> I will not be with those who are left here,
> I will be taken, when he fetches us here
> (Mbiti, 1971:53).

Often the conception of salvation as deliverance from evil, which we observed, is viewed as finalized and consummated in heaven at the return of Christ:

> Time is coming to an end, the kingdom is near;
> I believe in Jesus so that I may have life later.
> In the past I was in darkness, but now it is dawn:
> The great light is at God's home up above
> (Hymn 94, Mbiti, 1971:54).

Or this:

> When this life is over, when this life is over,
> We shall find furnished houses at Jesus' home,
> Which will be ours wherein to live [always]
> (Chorus 21, Ibid.)

The troubles of earth will be overcome:

> I know well when on earth
> My house is in heaven
> Our troubles and earthly joys shall end.
> My home is in heaven

> A nice fertile country where I shall enter
> There are no troubles but joy
>
> (Hymn 42; Mbiti, 1971:73).

One can certainly find support in Mbiti's contention that this emphasis does not provide encouragement for improving life on the earth. Perhaps there is something of the fatalism that we found was so prevalent in traditional Akamba faith. The tendency is to seek harmony, to go along with events, make the best of them, and Christians have simply carried this way of thinking with them.

On the one hand, there is no doubt something to this line of reasoning, and Mbiti may be putting his finger on a point where critical theology would begin to develop. On the other hand, it could be that this hope and this particular promise in the personal intervention of God is so outstanding and responds to such a deep-seated cultural need that, for the present, all other needs must be set aside. One thinks here of John V. Taylor's comment on the initial emphasis of African theology: "This discovery that the vague distant creator is the center and focus of every moment of all being is so catastrophic that it may overshadow for a time everything else in the Gospel" (1963: 122). So it would follow that the future appearance of this God to set right the disorder of the world would become a central focus of Akamba theology, whatever the abuses it might lead to.

This, then, is a sketch of some themes of an Akamba local theology. It is a faith with a keen sense of God's redeeming presence in the community. It focuses on the presence, and the future return, of the Lord of the church, Jesus Christ. While there are areas that remain undeveloped, at least at this reading—for example, the nature of forgiveness or a broader sense of Christian mission and vocation, it has raised issues that any theological reflection responding to this setting must address.

WORKS CITED

Mohammed Amin and Peter Moll.
  1983.   *Portraits of Africa.* London: Harvill.
Richard J. Gehman.
  1985.   *Ancestor Relations Among Three African Societies.*
           D.Miss. diss. Pasadena: Fuller Theological Seminary
           School of World Mission.
John S. Mbiti.
  1969.   *African Religions and Philosophy.* London: Heine-
           mann.

_____.

  1971.   *New Testament Eschatology in an African Back-
           ground.* Oxford: Oxford University.

_____.

  1986.   *The Bible and Theology in African Christianity.* Nai-
           robi: Oxford University.
'Zulu Sofola.
  1979.   "The Theatre in the Search for African Authenticity."
           In *African Theology En Route.* Edited by Kifi Appiah-
           Jubi and Sergio Torres. Maryknoll: Orbis.
John V. Taylor.
  1963.   *The Primal Vision: Christian Presence. and African
           Religions.* London: SCM.
Unpublished testimonies. Collected by Stanley Mutunga.

North America

NorthAmericaNorthA
ericaAmerica
orthNorthA
AmericaNorthA
ca
orthAmericaNorthA
ericaNorthAmerica
orthAmericaNorthA
ericaNorthAmerica
orthAmericaNorthA
ericaNorthAmerica
orthAmericaNorthA
ericaNorthAmerica

Chapter 6

An American Middle-Class Local Theology

Academic theologians in America have been notoriously reticent about making the religious experience of ordinary Christians the subject of sustained attention. As one put it in conversation recently: "There is a lot of craziness out there." Indeed there is! For evidence one need look no further than the Sunday supplement of the local newspaper. Just within the last few years we have seen a variety of relational theologies—what are called the health-and-wealth gospels—theologies focusing on positive thinking and self-esteem, to say nothing of influences from thinking that is lumped together under the rubric of New Age.

This proliferation of faiths, and their historical sources, has begun to receive serious attention by historians, producing studies that are not without influence in the project we are engaged in here (Randall Balmer, 1989; Jon Butler, 1990; and Nathan Hatch, 1989). But when theologians give this dimension of church life any attention it is usually assumed these things must simply be attacked and eliminated and replaced by reflection that is more solidly biblical.

The implications for the theologians' responsibility toward what are called lay people is clear: The reflection of ordinary Christians must simply be disciplined and corrected by the theological tradition. As we have argued, this is certainly one of the functions of theology. But perhaps theology has other, more preliminary roles to play. Here we want to ask a prior question: What is the cultural situation that has given rise to these informal theologies? And what then are the theological themes and practices that seem to commonly arise in this situation? In other words, what is the vernacular theology of the white American middle class? Our assumption is that these implicit frameworks and intuitions are to be treated with special respect—they are the houses in which people live day by day and they often display a surprising resilience and even a certain eloquence.

In the words Will Campbell borrows from Karl Barth, we will look at all Christians as "little theologians." By occupational choice, Campbell notes, he is neither a theologian nor a tractor mechanic. But in a way he is both.

> Yesterday I took the distributor cap off the old machine I had left in the snow and dried the condenser. The tractor still would not start, but in that act I became a mechanic. In the same fashion I have a neighbor, an electrician by occupation, who is a theologian. He told me he would not teach his child to pray "Now I lay me down to sleep. . ." because, he said, the words could be a reminder to God to put her on his agenda that night. That is a theological statement because it is a statement about the kind of God God is. My neighbor is a "little theologian," as Barth put it. And I am a little tractor mechanic (1984:42).

We want to discover, then, ways in which ordinary Christians are little theologians. Our method is to review the basic cultural values that define the world in which Americans live. Following this, we will listen to the narratives of a group of Christians, trying to discover the dominant themes and practices that embody their faith. This will put us in a position to make some general comments on the way a critical theology might proceed in America—one in which the people themselves will be major participants.

CULTURAL VALUES OF THE AMERICAN MIDDLE CLASS

From the time that the pilgrims fled to America in search of religious freedom, the relationship between America and Christianity has been as problematic as it has been intimate. Whether one believes that Christian values underlie the American democratic tradition, or that the secularization of that tradition has done much to corrupt the Christian church, it is clear that the cultural situation has had a large impact on what it means to be a Christian (the interested reader may refer to the book by Mark Noll, George Marsden, and Nathan Hatch, 1983, for a helpful summary of the issues).

In another place (Dyrness, 1989) I have spelled out what I believe are the major questions that Americans face in becoming faithful disciples. However, it is necessary here to review the major values that have developed before moving on to examine some dominant themes in a middle-class vernacular theology. Note that this generalized picture is subject to much qualification—both regionally and in terms of ethnic background. But it is possible to argue that in many ways white middle-class culture embodies and focuses on in a special way what characteristically are considered to be American values. As Robert Bellah and his colleagues argue: "We have stressed the special nature of the middle class, the fact that it is not simply a 'layer' in a system of stratification, but rather a group that seeks to embody in its own continuous progress and advancement the very meaning of the American project" (1985:151). Clearly, at least these values are typical of the group of Christians in Northern California that we study later in this chapter.

One might argue, in the first place, that Americans are *philosophically naturalistic.* Here we use philosophy in an informal sense of "way of life." This is to say that American life has been dominated by its natural, and later its artificial, environment. The physical challenges of the frontier in the Old West have become a theme not only of our literature and film, but also a metaphor for the challenges of life in general.

For most Americans practical demands regularly take precedent over more spiritual concerns. This means, on the one hand, that we are taught to be "self-reliant" as Ralph Waldo Emerson put it in the classic essay with that title. Ordinarily this means that we are able to confront the physical challenges we face, but it also has implications, as we will note, for the difficulty we have making and sustaining friendships. This complex of values puts a premium on skill and productivity, on what one can do or accomplish, and spends relatively little time reflecting carefully on the purposes for which things are done.

This means, on the other hand, that we tend to operationalize our values. Our "causes" are more reflective of our pragmatic desire to change the world than they are of our philosophical commitment to principles. We tend to measure success in physical or material terms rather than in social or religious ones. People are admired for what they can do or how much money they make rather than for the richness of their social or spiritual lives.

Finally, this tendency to work things out leads to a pervasive and sometimes debilitating naturalism. If life is primarily a series of physical challenges that I am responsible to meet, those areas of life that cannot be so understood— human weakness, suffering, and death—are simply and systematically ignored. God, when he exists, is there to help those who help themselves.

Americans, in the second place, are *psychologically humanistic.* For many Americans the primary goal of human life is seen in terms of individual and personal development. This means, on the one hand, that we pursue only those projects that contribute to the sense of personal fulfillment essential to our well-being. Americans are typically a generous people, ready to volunteer for any cause that promises to make a difference in the world, but they do so often to feel good about themselves.

On the other hand, this means that any project that seems to impede the opportunity for personal development is necessarily wrong and must be abandoned. A job, college major, or even a marriage partner failing to provide the expected opportunity for growth—the freedom for me to be who I am—must be exchanged for another that promises greater opportunity.

This group of values explains why, in Robert Bellah's words the language of individualism, coming perhaps from philosopher John Locke, has become the primary language for most Americans. As Bellah concludes: "What is good is what one finds rewarding. If one's preferences change, so does the nature of the good. Even the deepest ethical virtues are justified as matters of personal preference. Indeed, the ultimate ethical rule is simple that individuals should be able to pursue whatever they find rewarding" (1985:6). While this has contributed to an environment of freedom and opportunity, it has often impeded the development of any sense of social or public life to which I am responsible and that can contribute something to my identity.

Finally, the result of their narrow naturalism, which regularly ignores what cannot be put in problematic terms, and their humanism, which understands no limits to human potential, is that Americans are temperamentally optimistic. From the founding period of our country, Americans have felt themselves engaged in a special project. They believed they were a "city set on a hill" to which all the nations of the world would look for inspiration. Indeed, in the beginning they felt that God was with them in a special way, he had entered into a covenant with them, and this ensured the ultimate success of their venture.

Americans soon lost the sense of God's special involvement in their history—the Revolutionary War was a critical point—but they were unable to shake the optimism about their project. To this day, most Americans have the sense that, if they work hard, things will turn out all right in the end.

This hopefulness has encouraged Americans to tackle and sometimes accomplish projects that many would consider impossible. It has also led to a characterization by people of other nations that Americans are naïve and idealistic. In particular, this has led to an unusual commitment to freedom on the one hand, and an unwillingness to understand and embrace suffering on the other.   "APU Bubble"

The commitment of Americans to freedom is legendary—we fight wars, form governments and commit our resources in the name of freedom. This freedom has the special character of being defined over against tyrannies of all kinds. That is, freedom is always defined negatively in terms of being free from restrictions, it is rarely defined in positive terms of being free for something in particular. This view, with roots in the "real Whig" view of history, has played an enormous role not only in our national consciousness, but in our personal quests.

At the same time that we are committed to freedom and faith in the future, we are singularly unable to deal with personal failure or suffering. Our optimism leads to a large measure of denial, which is so characteristic of our corporate and personal lives. We have the idea that whatever problems we face, if we face them with a positive attitude and a dose of hard work, we can overcome them. Of course we soon learn that some problems are not solvable, at least not by thought and work alone. However, these problems can ordinarily be put out of our minds for awhile, certainly while we take another vacation in Europe.

These, then, are some of the fundamental values that drive us. They do not so much define our beliefs as provide the glasses by which we view the world. Getting outside of them and looking objectively at them is almost impossible—something like getting out and pushing the car in which we are riding. An attempt must be made, though, if we are to have some context for the narratives we explore below.

To complete the picture we ought to put these deeper values in the context of contemporary patterns of behavior in America. The values we have briefly examined might be seen as deep-seated orientations, which will be expressed in terms of changing attitudes. For example, a study done earlier this year by Princeton Survey Research Associates showed that 40 percent of Americans say that faith in God is the most important thing in life, far ahead of good health (29 percent) and a happy marriage (21 percent). This implies that the narcissistic era of the seventies and eighties may be giving way to a more spiritually sensitive generation. The research of George Barna supports this. In his recent book *The Frog in the Kettle* he argues that, at the same time momentum is against integrating religion into daily life, there is a growing tendency for people to develop *ad hoc* and highly personalized systems of faith. America may be post-Christian, but it may also be post-secular as well.

A LOCAL THEOLOGY FOR MIDDLE-CLASS AMERICANS

What themes and practices might be characteristic of Christians shaped by this cultural situation? To answer this question I have chosen a group of Christians in Northern California to interview. They belong to a fellowship group in a single church, and range in age from late twenties to early forties. Most are married with young children and have well-paying and relatively satisfying work situations. Through a series of personal interviews and by soliciting written narratives, during 1990 and 1991, I collected stories of their experiences with God, either at conversion, or during critical points in their lives. I wanted to learn how they typically speak of God. What is the language, the emphases, and practices that give expression to their faith in God? Reflection on their stories led to the following theological themes.

Conversion as a Fresh Beginning

It is no accident that being born again has become, for Americans, a synonym for being a real Christian. Whereas in many places in the world it is assumed one can be born into a Christian family or into a church parish, here, believing must be an act of personal choice. Often Christianity is spoken of as the opportunity for one to make a new start in life. As a result, Christians are often able to detail the time and place of their conversion experience—indeed for many it is important to "get the details right." One man testified: "It is very vivid in my memory the moment this happened. It stands out because it became so clear at that one point in time. It was an experience of acting on what I knew to be true in my own heart and mind." A women remembers a born-again experience in graduate school when she experienced a forgiving God. Another testified:

> I became a Christian just about 10 years ago, at the age of 26. It was a decisive event in my life, a turning point that has altered almost everything I do and say. I was a person who found a "God-shaped vacuum" inside myself that could be filled by nothing else. All other attempts at creating a fulfilling, happy life had been futile. My experimentation with drugs was making me paranoid and reclusive. I truly believe that I was saved from a self-destructive life and for relationship with a God who knows me and loves me.

Notable in this testimony is the reference to escape or deliverance from the past, which for many is the reverse of the need for a fresh start. Christianity, then, is understood in terms of God's active entrance into an individual's life, (usually) at a particular time, to deliver him or her from a past that was somehow oppressive. God's presence is clearly personal, we will have a great deal more to say about that, but it is also largely private and individualistic. Where other people figure in these stories, they appear as supporting actors; milestones on the way to an individual's liberation.

It follows that salvation, at least initially, is understood primarily in terms of a personal empowerment. People speak of finding themselves, or of feeling liberated; sometimes in moving language:

> I have never understood the power of confession, but to hold up the despair I have known was to know what freedom is. . . to confess your sins is to stand before God, naked in the spiritual sense, and say, "God give me strength to fulfill my mission in life." Perhaps this is what liberation is all about. . . . . Liberation is baring your soul before God and then pursuing your mission in life with faith and commitment.

Faith as Personal Relationship with God or with Christ

The most common language used to describe the life of faith, at least for this group, was the language of personal relationship. Entering into faith was sometimes spoken of as surrender. "I simply gave myself up," one described it, indicating that relationship with God is a matter of the will. Believing is often spoken of as commitment. "From the beginning of this journey of faith I have sensed God as an active part." "I have always felt God's presence in my life and have never doubted it." "I've described the experience since as having a physical feeling of God's Spirit inside me. It was like having a rod rammed down my spine, it was that tangible."

As we noted above, this presence is associated with a feeling of personal empowerment, or liberation. One woman teaches her children to pray to Jesus as the one who is always with them, and who frees them to love others. But the other side of this use of personal categories for faith is that problems in discovering or developing one's personal identity sometimes translate into problems of faith. One woman spoke about her faith as being currently in flux. Three years previously her father (a church elder) had died, and in working through her relationship with his Scottish sternness, she had not been able to come to terms with a loving and forgiving God. "In a sense," she said, "God died with my father. While intuitively I feel God in my life, I feel disenfranchised as a woman." Does God understand this? She is not sure.

A corollary of this personal dimension is the importance given to "quiet times" or "personal devotions," that is, to times when the personal dimension of faith can be intentionally nurtured. One spoke of being awakened to the need to read and study the Bible, another to the need for memorizing Scripture. Still another frequently sought a place to be alone—for him this meant hiking or camping in wilderness areas—where he could experience the presence of God.

> Nighttime. I am camped out under the stars. Orion is overhead and the moon is full. I am in the Kern River Valley. A dry semi-desert. The mountains rise up on each side of the valley and the snow on the mountains is luminous in the moonlight. This is a fitting close to one of those rare days where I find what peace on earth is really about.

In this case, the "God-shaped vacuum" that Americans feel is really the need for personal fulfillment and satisfaction. This language is so common to us that we do not notice how remarkable it is when placed with the language believers of other cultures have developed. Though we often speak positively of this as personal Christianity, indeed we are suspicious of those who cannot express their faith in these terms, sometimes faith becomes such a private experience it actually threatens our relations with others. The following account is a graphic example:

> I am very confused and lonely. I think that in my heart I need to have a means for spiritual growth and expression. I have that through printmaking. Now I am afraid to let my inner self speak. I am afraid that I might become obsessed with a passion that will consume me and possibly separate me from (my family). I am also afraid that if I don't let my inner self speak through printmaking that I might lose contact with my spiritual self, my feelings, and my emotions.

It is clear from this testimony that the value placed on the personal dimension—what Krister Stendahl has called the "introspective conscience of the West"—can be the means of anchoring Christianity firmly in one's inner world and making it real and vital. It can also become a kind of tyranny. Though personal faith becomes a great source of comfort for many people, at the same time, whatever cannot be vindicated at the bar of personal faith easily becomes expendable.

Christianity as a Means to Living a Better Life

For many people in the world, religion becomes a means for finding a "good life." Of course what counts as "good" is dependent on the values of a particular culture. We have seen that for many Americans a good life implies personal fulfillment. But as we saw earlier it also implies the ability to help us accomplish what we believe necessary. American Christians want a faith that works for them.

This may imply things as simple as God guiding one in the choices one makes, or being more open to people at work, or listening to others. One woman believes that Jesus helps her treat people with respect, because now she knows that there is someone there between them, someone bigger than both of them. As another testified:

> I truly believe that in following God's commands to me, I will be happy and satisfied. When times are difficult, I trust God to help me through them. He has provided me with friends, family, and many material blessings, and I try to serve him in all areas of my life.

On another level, a faith that works can contribute to the sense that one's life can make a difference in the world. Sometimes, when associated with the gifts of the Spirit, this is part of the desire to discover one's mission in life. "I am committed to making a difference in the lives of people. . .and together I believe we can make a difference in how we view this planet and humanity."

In some areas of America this desire to see faith made real

is manifest in the desire for what is called "victorious Christianity," whose roots are in the Keswick Bible Conference movement of the end of the last century. A similar emphasis in some forms of California Christianity features positive thinking and a focus on self-esteem. While there seemed to be no direct influence on the group I spoke with, these ideas were not absent altogether, as is evident from the following testimony:

> Part of what I have learned in the past year is the power of the words I speak. I still play the silly games of dreaming and wishing, but when I really see something to which I can commit myself I can cut through the wishing and speak the words that bring forth action. Yesterday I was in a busy part of [town], as I drove to a client I said, "There will be a place to park when I get to the front of the building." The space was yellow, but I only needed to stop for two minutes. In this sense we truly are created in God's image.

The danger, of course, is that God and faith can become merely instrumental to my purposes, rather than my life being subordinated to the purposes of God. But for most Christians there is simply a quiet sense, a "childlike trust" as one woman put it, that God is there and will take care of us. That woman recalled a time when she had a phone call telling about her father's heart attack. She remembers the assurance God gave her that her father was in God's hands and would be saved. For this person, in fact, it did not seem that faith had been conceived in a complex and abstract way. Rather it was lived out in the practicalities of life as a wife and mother of two small children. Her life is lived under pressures, she testified, it is impossible to find quiet times. So she prays often for God's help in the midst of the demands of a busy life. And through it all God has taken care of her.

Centrality of Small Fellowship Groups

We have noticed that a weakness of an emphasis on personal faith is that *personal* can become *private*, and the public and social character of faith can be lost sight of. To a certain extent, this problem has been addressed in American Christianity by an emphasis on developing small groups. Small groups that meet for Bible study and prayer or merely for Christian fellowship are the unique social expression of personal Christianity.

Our sources expressed a very common American frustration with finding a church home. One mentioned "struggling to find a church," another testified that "it was more than six months before I finally found my way to church." But all, in one way or another, echoed the desire to connect with others: "I need to have connection to a group." Some see this as a kind of emotional closeness: "closer than my own family." Others look to a group for encouragement to live the Christian life. When the one who had spent six months looking finally found a group, he reported "the sincerity and rigorousness of their faith in God and in Jesus Christ was an inspiration and model for me."

But for all, the experience of a group becomes, in one way or another, an extension of the personal faith they have found in Christ. The way the group can become a foil for individual growth and development becomes clear in this narrative:

> My Christian house was built on the rock of Christ, one Christian wrote, but it was very small at the start. Now it is a "fortress built from the love and support of friends. One year ago I started a project called *growing friends*. At the time, I had no idea how I was going to grow friends. All I know is that I said I was committed to having a group of thirty people worldwide that would support me in my projects. Not just casual friends, but a strong family of people with strong and lasting commitments. . . . People seem to show up the strongest when I see an opportunity to contribute to their lives. It is a paradox. When I contribute to people, they support me in ways I never dreamed of."

Whether the group fulfills a need to serve others, or is simply there for their support, it serves in any case a particularly personal role in the lives of its members. Small groups have become the practice most characteristic of what is called evangelical Christianity.

This limited selection of themes and practices may give some idea of the shape of theological understanding in this community. Other practices could be mentioned, but they would only be adding details to a picture that is generally clear. A further example might be attitudes and practices involving the giving of money to Christian causes. Several comments led me to believe that, unlike Christians in most developing countries, for American Christians, giving money is a means of demonstrating their trust in God. Rather than holding it tightly, we give it away because God will take care of us. In poorer countries one trusts God in order to get things that are needed. Giving, then, would be a more sacrificial expression of gratitude. But in both cases these practices reflect the different attitudes toward God's presence and care, and they must be understood in the light of those frameworks. For the North American, the personal presence of God is not automatically associated with the meeting of physical needs. These are ordinarily met as a matter of course, and dependence on God is something to be cultivated. For the Christian in a poor country, a day-to-day dependence on God is fundamental to faith, and the personal language we find so central may seem less important. Though clearly both groups have things to learn, is one faith perspective more biblical than the other?

A CONTEXTUAL THEOLOGY OF CHRIST AND SALVATION AND A CRITICAL PERSPECTIVE

Our challenge, then, is to ask how the process of critical development might take place for this local theology. We will do this by first making some general comments about the structure of the understanding of Christianity we have described. Here we will take the liberty of generalizing from the case we have studied. Then we will seek to describe the theology of Christ and salvation that is implicit in this understanding. Finally, as a step toward developing a critical perspective, we will seek to describe what we have called a central paradigm of thought—in this case a paradigm story— that collects and centers some of the major themes surveyed.

Clearly, the Americans we have heard from are without exception on a quest for personal meaning. Their experience with God does not relate to social or political issues—these are not pressing to them as they are, say, to believers in Latin America. Nor does it relate to problems associated with finding food or shelter, or with recurrent illness—unlike their counterparts in parts of Africa, they are not ordinarily confronted with urgent physical needs. Their need is entirely related to personal questions of meaning and satisfaction. The God-shaped vacuum has this contour, and their encounter with God in Jesus Christ has met this fundamental need. In a typical expression one person summed up his joy at discovering "the incomparable satisfaction of living life as a Christian."

Moreover this quest and its satisfaction is described almost entirely in an "I" language rather than a "we" language. Other people figure in their stories, sometimes quite prominently, but they do so as ancillary to the central drama of personal meaning. There is an underlying desire to connect and have relationships with others. But these links must always be forged, often from scratch. They are not assumed. Unlike most Third-World cultures that start with the community and find identity within the group, Americans feel the need to find themselves individually, first, and then use groups to express an already formed self.

American Christianity is not without its rituals and practices, but its character is shaped by this central quest for personal and individual meaning. Any ritual in worship, however rich in historical or theological meaning, if not found to be personally meaningful, will not survive. As a result, rituals are as different as the people who practice them. We have seen that small-group fellowships are central to American Christianity, but the shape they take is as different as the people who take part in them.

This is because rituals must also express the individual preferences of the people. The weight of tradition, what we often disparage as habit, while not missing altogether, is often actively resisted. This means that our rituals often have an *ad hoc* character. Each person we spoke to had his or her own set of personal or family practices that they had developed to express and nurture their faith—walking in the wilderness, breathing quick prayers, and meeting with Christian friends in various ways. This, of course, is characteristic of the wider American church. Wedding vows in California churches are often rewritten by the participants to express their own view of things. In fact, in ceremonies of this kind there is a certain pressure to "be creative" and "express your real feelings." Worship services are adapted to fit changing expectations.

Contemplating this picture of faith, must we draw the common conclusion that this is a faith that has capitulated to the broader values of American society? James Davison Hunter, for example, worries about what he calls the cognitive dissonance of evangelicalism and modernity. As a result of this dissonance he sees a subtle and progressive erosion of belief. In particular, he focuses on three activities that he believes are essential for spiritual growth: Bible reading, prayer, and public testimony. He believes that under the influence of the culture these have been made into formulas. He concludes: "Whether this cultural accommodation will eventually result in a doctrinal compromise remains to be seen" (1983:101).

Our sample certainly gives some evidence in support of his fears. The practices he notes did not appear central to any of our group, and it is not hard to argue that there is no widely shared understanding of the major doctrines—at least this does not play a major role in their lives. In fact, there does not seem to be much concern for any objective foundation underlying their vital experiences with Christ. Interestingly this group has been exposed to regular biblical teaching, some even in a formal graduate setting. But somehow that teaching did not seem to connect with their lives.

It can also be argued that there is a definite, if sometimes tacit, understanding of Christ's person and work. One person said: "I look at the despair that I have known and the burden of trying to carry my own failings on my shoulders and then I look at Christ, who bore the sins of men [sic]. What despair did he experience?" Or another: "Even at the early age of twelve, I understood that God loved me and sent Jesus to die to pay the price for my sins. I had a strong sense of right and wrong and a strong desire to do what God wanted me to do."

For them, Jesus is the central figure of their spiritual lives. One referred to him as being a role model, though she also admitted that she had not really been able to pick up on the Cross and its meaning. Another spoke of Christ as the way God had broken through to him. Another believes that even at the age of six the Holy Spirit had called her to follow Christ with her life.

The salvation Christ brings has to do with the discovery of personal meaning as we noted. "I was a person who found a 'God-shaped vacuum' inside myself that could be filled by nothing else. All other attempts at creating a fulfilling, happy life had been futile. . . . I truly believe that I was saved *from* a self-destructive life and *for* a relationship with a God who knows me and loves me." This vision of the good life may be limited by the expectations that this culture has given them, but it is clear that God has broken in and met them in terms of these expectations.

Robert Johnston has recently argued that Americans have rejected traditional understandings of Christ's work, not because of any anti-religious bias, but because "they lack any strong cultural model for understanding it" (1988:210). Traditionally, he points out, the Atonement has been described almost exclusively in the language of accountability. Americans no longer understand this language, having replaced it with the language of fulfillment. We have seen evidence for the truth of his conclusion that "it is the imagery of family life and of restored relationship that holds the greatest initial promise for effective communication today" (Ibid., 212).

Two further aspects of our case study may be pointed out in this connection. First, there seems no doubt that these people have had a definite encounter with a living God in the person of Christ. For some, the experience was more dramatic than for others, but all were quite emphatic, and some even lyrical, about this experience and its significance. God had "liberated" or "met" them in some definite way, often in the context of decisive and life-changing circumstances.

Second, they have associated this experience with the events of the life and death of Jesus Christ. Here they are perhaps less articulate than we would like them to be, but they do have a conviction that somehow the life of Christ is decisive for their lives and for their salvation.

What do we make of the picture of faith we have sketched? If we follow the axiom that the critical perspective must arise from within the group in question, it may not be helpful to simply point out the weaknesses of the picture that emerges. Rather than criticizing the point at which they find themselves, it seems far more important to meet them at that point and see how they might be moved further in the process of Christian growth. They are, after all, people on the way, like we all are. Moreover their expressions of faith have the ring of authenticity to them. They understand that Jesus is a role model, they depend on him, but they are struggling to relate this to what he did on the Cross. It strikes me that it is people very much like these to whom Paul wrote his letters. Those called theologians may be struggling at different points, but we would be deceiving ourselves if we did not admit that our struggles, in the end, are very much like those we have described here. We all need the same grace.

This critical process might be taken a step further by trying to discover a central paradigm of thought, what we might call a paradigm story, that defines the spiritual thrust of American culture. In the summer issue of *The Quality Review* (1988), James Lader discusses the search for quality in

American business. The conglomerate AT&T, in order to discover how Americans felt about quality, hired Gilbert Rapaille as a consultant to interview groups of employees about the concept. Analyzing recurring themes and words, Rapaille developed a profile of American attitudes that he used to develop a paradigm story.

Quality for Americans, Rapaille soon saw, is an emotionally laden concept. Programs in search of "zero defects" or "doing it right the first time" were viewed negatively because they implied the possibility of defeat. They stimulated the fear that one has no worth in the eyes of those who matter. Quality improvement however would be viewed positively if it were associated with change, innovation, and the possibility of a breakthrough. "Americans need to believe not in the perfectibility of existing products but in the unconstrained possibilities of quantum leaps of progress" (Lader, 1988:34).

Most interesting for our purposes was what Rapaille called the dominant imprinting story that Americans carry around with them. He describes this as follows:

> The child is with other children and adults. He/she is feeling okay. She has something to do, and is not unaware of difficulties of the task, but she is happy to try it. She does something that does not fit the adult expectations. She cries, is upset, ashamed, and realizes she did not know exactly what to do. Somebody is there. . .they say, "It's all right that you made a mistake. I care about you, because you are somebody special and I trust you. I'm sure you are going to get better." The child tries again and eventually succeeds. She feels good about what has happened. She is proud of succeeding, of having overcome the difficulties (Lader, 1988:35).

In this story, Rapaille identifies a lawgiver who communicates the seriousness of the situation in which the first attempts to succeed inevitably fail. Then there is the mentor who provides the sympathetic encouragement to overcome the obstacles and succeed.

Americans readily identify with a story of this kind—it is repeated in a hundred forms in our classic literature or in film. One might inquire as to whether this story has not already undergone some Christian influence. Erich Auerbach has argued along these lines in his classic study of Western literature (1953). He believes our idea of story, with a beginning, middle, and end—climax and anticlimax—has been indelibly marked by the Christian story of redemption. Be that as it may, the story we have isolated lays down the lines and defines the language that salvation, at least initially, may be understood in the American context.

Clearly, this story matches well with the quest for personal meaning that, for our respondents, has been satisfied by an encounter with Christ. It is a story in which the language of accountability, to use Robert Johnston's words, has been integrated into the language of fulfillment and relationship. But there are ways in which even their interpretation of the faith transcends this American story. When confronted with this story they would point out that the success of their faith is ultimately because of God's intervention; it is not merely a matter of their overcoming obstacles. Moreover, there is a clear understanding that though Jesus is a kind of mentor, he is much more than that. He is God, the deliverer.

Upon hearing this story there would doubtless be a recognition that this set of expectations does threaten, from time to time, to shape Americans' understanding of Christianity. Christ is sometimes used instrumentally in support of my projects. He is pressed into service as a sympathetic mentor, a helper, and not allowed to play the role of Lord of Lords. In this they would see that they share, more generally, some of the weakness of American Christianity.

What can be done to move people beyond this level of understanding? How can this insight into their experience be used to nudge them in the direction of maturity? Though this aspect must necessarily be brief, we have implied that there are two ways that a "critical theology" may be encouraged.

The first way is to discipline the thinking that is done here by comparing it with certain conceptual categories developed in Western theology. One example of this may be to take the classical discussion of the nature of Christ, one person with two natures, and compare it with the understanding of Christ implicit in these testimonies. Is an emphasis on Christ as "role model" overplaying his humanity? What is the significance of his divinity in relation to his death? Perhaps making explicit what they are saying in their narratives would put them in a position to "hear" what others have said about Christ's person and work.

This has obvious merit and is the preferred way of theological instruction. But there is a second way in which the critical process can be encouraged. That is, one may confront these stories, this set of practices, with another story and another set of practices. Let us say after examining the paradigm story of the little girl that we study the parable of the Prodigal Son (Luke 15:11–31). There the brother is not encouraged to overcome some obstacle, but has to realize his total helplessness. It is the father who does everything for him—welcomes him, gives him a robe, prepares a celebration for him, and even works to reconcile him with his older brother. All the younger son has to do is return to the waiting father (which is really a better title for the parable), and celebrate the reunion. Perhaps Americans confronted with this story will realize that "coming to oneself in a far country" is not the same thing as "finding personal meaning," and that, however important that latter quest is, it is nothing compared with going home to the father and making merry with the family.

WORKS CITED

Erich Auerbach.
    1953.   *Mimesis: The Representation of Reality in Western Literature.* Princeton: Princeton University.

Randall Balmer.
    1989.   *Mine Eyes Have Seen the Glory: A Journey into the Evangelical Subculture in America.* Oxford: Oxford University.

George Barna.
    1990.   *The Frog in the Kettle.* Ventura: Regal.

Robert Bellah, Richard Masden, William M. Sullivan, Ann Swidler, and Steven M. Tipton.
    1985.   *Habits of the Heart: Individualism and Commitment in American Life.* Berkeley: University of California.

Jon Butler.
    1989.   *Awash in a Sea of Faith: Christianizing the American People.* Cambridge, Mass.: Harvard University.

Will D. Campbell.
    1984.   "Nit-picking on a Fine Book." *Christianity and Crisis.* 44/2. (February): 42–43.

William Dyrness.
    1989.   *How Does America Hear the Gospel.* Grand Rapids: Eerdmans.

Douglas W. Frank.
    1986.   *Less Than Conquerors: How Evangelicals Entered the Twentieth Century.* Grand Rapids: Eerdmans.

Nathan Hatch.
    1989.   *The Democratization of American Christianity.* New Haven: Yale University.

James Davison Hunter.
    1983.   *American Evangelicalism, The Coming Generation.* New Brunswick: Rutgers University.

Robert K. Johnston.
    1988.   "Acculturation or Inculturation? A Contemporary Evangelical Theology of the Atonement." *Covenant Quarterly.* 46:200–214.

James I. Lader.
    1988.   "Getting Emotional About Quality." *The Quality Review*, (Summer): 32–36.

Mark Noll, Nathan Hatch, and George Marsden.
    1983.   *The Search for Christian America*. Westchester, Ill.: Crossway.

Krister Stendahl.
    1976.   "The Apostle Paul and the Introspective Conscience of the West." In *Paul Among Jews and Gentiles*. Philadelphia: Fortress.

Conclusion

Chapter 7

Conclusion: Cross-Cultural Dialogue as Theological Conversation

We began this study by recalling the grand image of John the Evangelist from Revelation 7 where people from "all nations, and kindreds, and people, and tongues" join in singing praise to the Lamb (v. 9, KJV). In the interim we have listened to a few of these peoples and the particular praise that they have been moved to give. Of course this is only the merest beginning—people from hundreds of other tribes would just as eagerly have given their tribute to God's working in their lives.

This sample, though, has given us a sense of how the Gospel has made its way into the most intimate details of people's lives. While occasionally we have noted the influence of missionaries in this process, in the end, we sense that we are in the presence of something larger than simply a missionary movement. What we are witnessing of course is the Spirit of God calling out a people from among the nations. According to the Christian view, this process is the meaning of this period of history—what the New Testament calls the end of the age. As Lesslie Newbigin describes this: "It is in the mercy of God that the final unveiling of his power is held back so that all nations may have the same opportunity that was given to the first hearers in Galilee, the opportunity to repent, to be converted, and to believe and recognize the presence of the reign of God in the crucified Jesus" (1989:106).

Our particular interest in these groups is in the way they are beginning the process of theological reflection. In the introduction we focused on this pursuit in two ways. First, we noted that some of the most significant theological development takes place among people with little or no formal theological education—indeed often with little education of any kind. By getting people to tell the story of God's intervention in their lives we tried to find out how their particular understanding of God has developed.

Stories, we argued, are crucial to a people's dignity and self-understanding. The Bible is filled with stories revealing God's purposes and character. Though the stories we have used are those of individuals, they often reflect broadly held convictions. In fact, as one theologian put it recently, these Christians are making a claim about an emerging pattern in the world. William Placher goes on to say that "Christian readers of the Bible find in the pattern of Jesus' life a pattern that recurs again and again elsewhere in the Bible, in extra-biblical history, and in their own lives" (1989:127). We have surveyed some of the ways this pattern has been traced.

This leads us to the second aspect of our focus. We have tried to broaden the typical Western understanding of theology as sure knowledge to include the practices and symbols by which vernacular theology is articulated. We have been working with the assumption that theology is the framework by which Christians structure their lives. This certainly includes explicit understandings of God and Christ, but it also includes practices that have grown out of a people's central convictions that may be only partially understood.

Moreover, we have acknowledged that this is a developing framework, reflecting the people's growing experience with God and their growing understanding of that experience—reflecting their growth into maturity in Christ. The roles we have defined for the theologian have been that of an observer (sometimes from outside the community), and, as far as possible, a facilitator of this process. But we were careful to insist that the people themselves must own the process and that the critical dimension should develop within the community, even if the outsider is sometimes the occasion for this development.

In this conclusion we will make some summary comments that reflect further on this development. First, we will ask: How do theological convictions function—or, in some cases, fail to function—in the cases we have studied? Following this, we will briefly consider the implications of this for the way we think about and teach theology. Finally, we will conclude by taking one aspect of theology—what is sometimes called a theology of spirituality—to use as an example of theological discussion among the peoples we have studied.

THE DEVELOPMENT OF CRITICAL THEOLOGY

We have argued that theological frameworks, even if they are partially (or largely) implicit, can still be subject to critique. But we have insisted that, to have an impact on the people, the critique must be developed and understood within the community. Let us elaborate this point further. On one level, the very entrance of the Gospel into the life of an individual or a people is a critique of old ways of thinking and living. The Gospel has given Chinese Christians the courage to resist the dictates of their government; it has given Mam Christians a way to transcend barriers between Indian and Ladino culture, and so on.

But there must be no illusion that, even in Christian communities, all will go well as people obey the Gospel. Obedience is a part of our hermeneutics, or our interpretation, of Christian truth. Therefore, as with all interpretation, it will necessarily be distorted by personal or cultural factors. Even as

we admire the faith of other people, we must avoid romanti-
cizing their Christianity. Certainly we will want to learn from
them, but we do not go to them assuming their way of
believing God is automatically better than ours. As Clifford
Geertz put this, we must avoid believing that foreign wisdom
"is a prosthetic for a damaged spirituality" (1983:44).

We have also stressed that viewing frameworks compara-
tively allows these traditions to mutually confront each other,
one highlighting what another overlooks. But this is not to
imply that the weakness we see in one or another community
doesn't matter because other groups are strong at that point.
As Richard Mouw makes this point: "If a specific group has a
weak grasp of the reality of God's Trinitarian workings, then I
would be inclined to encourage them to improve their
theology and practice on this point, rather than viewing their
imbalance as a helpful corrective to the larger ecclesial whole"
(1990:154).

What we must avoid assuming is that there is some ideal
standard of faith that can be applied equally to all. In fact, it is
the larger ecclesial whole that often points out the weaknesses
in the first place. Let us illustrate by taking Mouw's reference
to a group's grasp of God's Trinitarian working. From the
sources we have seen of a Mam local theology, which are
certainly incomplete, we have found very little reference to
the Holy Spirit. In some ways, in fact, the Godhead seems to
be Christ and the Father, with the Holy Spirit not visibly
active as God in the believers' lives. Assuming for the
moment that this is an accurate picture of Mam theology (and
might we say of other evangelical theologies of Latin America?), one could say that the explosive growth of Pentecostal-
ism in Latin America is an implicit critique of this theological
weakness. Charismatic groups have discovered a dimension of
faith that other groups have ignored, and even their excesses
may point to lacunae in neighboring local theologies.

So there is a sense in which the entrance of the Gospel is
itself a "critical moment" in the life of a people—old ways are
challenged, new vistas open up; and the encounter with others

sometimes offers a critical perspective that points up areas of weakness. Even so, are there other directions in which a critical dimension may be developed in the cases we have studied? Perhaps as a start in answering this important question we could point to three areas of potential development.

First, it seems obvious to one trained in Western theology that these groups, even the American sample, have a relatively *undeveloped sense of historical perspective.* While traditions are extremely important they are often limited to a tribal memory or to community stories. The people often do not see how these traditions can be put into any larger world historical picture. Thus, while Chinese Christians are moved to tears when they hear about prayers being offered for them by fellow believers around the world, they do not reflect on what these relationships mean historically—what they were before the revolution and what might become of them in the future. In the case of the Manila squatters, we saw evidence that the historical dimension had been swallowed up almost entirely by the symbolic dimension, and in the American sample, by personal identity issues.

And yet, even here, we saw evidence that the Gospel was the means for initiating movement in the direction of historical thinking. The important and moving case of the Indian and Ladino confrontation over land use and ownership, and the spirit of innovation that Indian farmers often display, gives important evidence that a people can begin to free themselves from bondage to natural cycles and situations of oppression. The case of the Akamba was particularly interesting. Part of the transformation of the Gospel for them lay, almost literally, in a transfer of temporal focus from the past to the future. Rather than seeing the key to understanding (and affecting) the present by way of the past through ancestor worship, they began to look ahead to the return of Christ and life in heaven with God (and their relatives) as the key to a good life.

A second area of potential development for these theological frameworks is in regard to the *relative absence of any tradition of critical thought*. Here, again, I do not mean to emphasize only a Western way, as though all groups need to develop the same sense of abstract thinking and reflection. But we might ask: What is it that allows a people to have a critical perspective toward themselves, to be able to look at their situation with some objectivity while probing weaknesses and encouraging strengths? We saw that the attitude of Chinese Christians toward government was entirely understandable and even justified in the present circumstances. But the present situation of Christians in Eastern Europe, where government hostility is giving way to tentative encouragement, suggests that attitudes toward government be defined far less dogmatically than Chinese Christians in the house churches are doing. And where is the voice that will speak against the excesses of the fiestas and processions of Catholics in Metro Manila? Or against the danger of psychologizing the faith by American Christians?

The critical dimension we intend to point out is really an exercise of the biblical role of prophecy within the body of Christ. In Scripture it is the prophet who speaks for God regarding the affairs of people and nations, and it is the prophet who is able to have a sense of distance from the political and social pressures at work in the world. Lesslie Newbigin, in fact, has recently argued that the entire tradition of rational thought has its roots in the biblical story and especially in the voice of the prophet speaking on behalf of God. The structure of this tradition, he believes, has a narrative character and is based on what he calls the logic of election. It takes the personal calling of "Moses as its starting point and continues through the succeeding millennia into the present day in various forms, Jewish, Christian, and Islamic" (1989:60, 74, 99, 152).

There seems little doubt that it is the Judeo-Christian tradition of prophecy that lies behind the Western tradition of critical thought—even the most complex modern forms as seen in Marx, Nietzsche, and Freud. However, this does not imply that the Judeo-Christian tradition of thinking must therefore become normative for all peoples, as Newbigin seems to suggest. Election, and the story of Christ, for example, will become decisive for the thinking of all people, but they will have their own special impact on the various cultures they encounter.

Third, the people, in certain of the cases that we reviewed, had the tendency *to understand Christian truth functionally rather than substantially.* Even in the brief allusions we made to traditional faiths, we saw that these faiths often were essentially utilitarian in character. In Mayan religion, the rituals are meant to orient life around the fundamental temporal and spatial structures of life so that things will continue to go well. In Akamba traditional religion, illness or famine reflect a disturbance coming from the realm of the spirits that must be dealt with by proper sacrificial intervention. God (or the gods) are to be invoked rather than worshipped. In America, we saw how the pragmatic orientation of its culture often led to a search for a faith that works.

Here, again, the biblical notion of worship as honoring the transcendent God by recalling his goodness stands as a unique and purifying notion. In certain of our cases this idea was beginning to emerge. In China, for example, testifying to Jesus, that is, recounting his goodness, has become a central element of their worship experiences. For the Mam, honoring the Lord Christ has taken over a central place in their religious practice, but, even here, following Christ is tied significantly to obedience to his Word. As one Mam believer put it: "What is it that Dios (God) observes in our behavior? How does Kman Crist (the Lord Christ) look on us? Are we doing what we do with joy? Do we go quickly and do what Kman Dios has told us to do?" (Quoted in Scotchmer, 1989:301).

What we see, then, is the Gospel working its way into a context where utility of faith is prominent—until the idea of the glory and honor of God as he is in himself begins to displace all other considerations. An illustration is provided by the Akamba case. There a worldview in which a multitude of powers threaten the people has been supplanted by one in which God alone exercises power through his Son. It would stand to reason that prayer would become a prominent means of worship as believers appeal to God as the single sustainer of their life. Previously, as Kwame Bediako notes of a similar West African situation, power was broadly refracted and religious activity had to be directed in many directions. Now God's saving power focuses on Christ: "Christ assumes the roles of all these points of our piety which we addressed to various sources of power" (1983:117). Power issues still dominate, but now their focus is on Christ. Worship patterns would change, then, from a focus on manipulation and control to one of intercession, and finally praise.

In all three of these areas of weakness—historical perspective, critical thinking, and instrumental understanding of faith—we can see ways in which the entrance of the Gospel is the decisive element. In each case, whatever the strengths or weaknesses of background traditions, the encounter with the living God in and through the work of his Son Jesus becomes the first step in opening these critical dimensions. It is the fact of Jesus' life and death and the central hope of his return that becomes a key to a developing historical sense. It is the transcendent Word of God through the prophets that allows people to develop a critical distance from themselves and is the key to development of critical thought. It is finally that greatness and glory of God that draws our worship in spite of the urgent needs that first moved us to prayer.

Of course, none of this is as clear in these cases as perhaps we would like it to be. However, once again we have to say that authentic spiritual life and growth are like this. We are all on a journey of faith, and understanding and theological reflection is meant to illumine that journey not replace it. We commented earlier that a theological framework is a part of our interpretation, and therefore is subject to all the personal and cultural distortions to which these understandings are always subject.

One of the weaknesses that we have not yet discussed is the absence of any sustained or systematic reflection on Scripture in any of the narratives we reviewed. What we did see is that, in various ways, Scripture does play a central role in these cases, with the exception perhaps of the Manila squatters. True, Scripture's importance does not seem to translate into the kind of study to which we aspire in our Western context, but, I would like to argue, its message and substance is, in fact, central to the faiths we have surveyed. Moreover, I believe it is fair to say that the entire developing framework is a kind of hermeneutical exercise in which this Scripture is being interpreted. As Richard Muller points out in his recent study of the nature of theology, historical criticism is nothing less than the understanding of Christianity in past linguistic and cultural situations. Similarly, present-day efforts to contextualize the faith are an adaptation of Christian teaching to new linguistic and cultural situation. "Contextualization, therefore, when it is a conscious exercise, is part of a historically controlled exercise in hermeneutics" (1991:205). But this hermeneutics, or method of interpretation, will vary greatly according to its setting, which leads us to our next question: What does this imply for the study and teaching of theology?

IMPLICATIONS FOR THE STUDY AND TEACHING OF THEOLOGY

Hermeneutics, or the science of interpretation, has become a central concern (some might even say an obsession) of Western theology during the past two decades. Theologians have been anxious to outline principles of interpreting Scripture as a means of avoiding the extreme subjectivism that often characterizes modern thought. However carefully these principles are articulated though, most theologians have come to accept Rudolph Bultmann's famous thesis that "exegesis without presupposition is impossible." (1960; For a general recent discussion of developments see Lundin, et al., 1985.)

Everyone approaches the text with ideas about the world and history that have influenced their reading of Scripture. These ideas can change, of course, but their presence must be recognized. In the common practice of translating North American (or European) textbooks on hermeneutics into other languages in very different cultural situations we are in danger of a very subtle kind of imperialism. What we are implying in this export of textbooks is that the presuppositions we use in reading Scripture must be used by others, even though their situations and picture of the world may be very different. It is of course possible for, say, Africans to read texts written by British scholars and learn from them—indeed reading these texts might play a crucial role in calling attention to the differences and stimulating similar reflection on the African situation—but this will only be a healthy process if they keep in mind the very different situations of the writer, and intended readers of the text.

One of the things that has become clear in our study is the situational and communal character of the theological frameworks that emerged. As I read the stories of these believers, time and again I found myself saying: "Of course, they would say that given their situation." It is easy enough for us to become impatient with the overemphasis on images and symbols among the Manila squatters. But given the shape of their imagination and their special history, it would be hard to conceive of a spirituality in which these things did not play an important role.

These reflections, then, inevitably lead us to conclude that the process of theological growth, and therefore the nature of theological education, must begin at the point where the people find themselves. Theological reflection, we have emphasized, will not become uncritical or romantic about other traditions, but it will honor the situated character of the interpretive process.

Traditional theological education, as it has developed in

the West, places a large emphasis on the reading and interpretation of texts, supremely the written text of Scripture and texts written about Scriptures (i.e., imagine a study of the Bible that did not focus on the endless production of commentaries). Moreover, the preferred exercise in which these texts are studied is in the students' writing—in other words, in the production of more texts. Now, this method has worked well in societies that are highly literate, but it works less well in societies where authority resides, say, in traditions embodied in a group of elders and their oral narratives. How would theological education proceed in a society whose social and religious life is oriented around fiestas honoring local saints, or where the whole of their religious practice must be underground? In the one case, texts are, at least initially, unavailable; in the other, they are forbidden.

The partial answer to theological growth that we have proposed is that theological education might proceed by recording and reflecting on the stories people tell of God's intervention in their lives. It is conceivable that certain of these stories, say of a great Christian leader, might become the "normative theological text" for the next generation of leaders, because it will reflect what she or he cares deeply about and therefore show what is valued by the community. It will also show how God has dealt with this people. As the Bible contains archetypical stories that make people show up as storied—as people with a destiny involving God and redemption—so our lives can take a similar shape, a pattern of this Pattern. What Patricia Benner says of the role of stories in the healing arts, applies as well to theological development. "Those who would heal, help, and minister also require story. To tell a story one must have a sense of importance, what is worth telling and in what order. To tell stories is to participate in meanings and extend them. To be a person living in a meaningful world is evidenced by having a story and the ability to tell a story" (1991).

We have seen as well how these stories often came to focus on some seminal practice or symbolic structure—worship, singing, or prayer. We saw, too, that these can only be partially captured by our verbal descriptions and explanations, which showed up another weakness of traditional text-centered theological education. It is strong on the cognitive and reflective, but gives less room for development of nonverbal dimensions of the faith.

In fact, we might go further and say that, in the Protestant examples we surveyed, Christianity has played a central role in what sociologists call demystification or rationalization. Dimensions of mystery or of symbols have often been eliminated in favor of verbal icons—remember the totems of traditional Mayan faith and the fragments of Scripture that replaced them on the walls of the homes of Christian Mam. In the case of American evangelicalism this slimming down of symbolism has left hardly any space for ritual of any kind.

Yet our focus on a framework of practices as well as on beliefs has given significant indication that the symbolic dimension may still play a role. Who can forget, for example, the moving description of people lining the river bank in preparation for early baptisms among the Kamba? Who can forget the accounts of believers recently released from prison in China, which often became a central form of testimony (which recalls the central and symbolic role that persecution played in the first three centuries of church history)? These and other elements move us further in the direction of a broader conception of theological education, one that will certainly do nothing to discourage the production and use of texts and written reflection, but will seek to supplement these with other symbolic structures—narratives, symbols, and ritual practices.

CROSS-CULTURAL SPIRITUALITY

It might be useful to conclude with a brief reference to a single theological issue, what we call spirituality, or Christian living, as an example of the way a cross-cultural dialogue might proceed. We noted in the introduction that one of the obvious facts of theological reflection in the West is that growth in precision of understanding has not been matched by a corresponding vitality of faith and Christian experience. Some might argue in fact that there is an inverse correlation between these things.

To our comments earlier, we might add those of A. W. Tozer who believes "the church has surrendered her once lofty concept of God" and with "the loss of a sense of majesty has come the further loss of religious awe and consciousness of the divine Presence" (Quoted in Muller, 1991:216). In fact, this loss has come at precisely the point at which, outwardly, our churches are prospering.

Meanwhile, almost without exception, the stories we heard from elsewhere in the world recounted a lively sense of God's presence. Even among the Manila squatters there is a dramatic trust in God's goodness. In Guatemala the joy of salvation focuses on the deliverance that the Lord Christ has brought about over the "lord of sin," or evil persons. There, spirituality clearly takes on a political dimension whereby even the oppressive social structure has been impacted by the lordship of Jesus.

Among Christians in the house churches, the very real physical risks have encouraged a dependence on God that people in less vulnerable circumstances can only imagine.

> Every Christian has a straw mat at home. Whenever they run into any difficulty they kneel down and pray. When the brothers and sisters see each other, they seldom talk about how they are and what has happened and so forth [instead] they kneel down and pray. Thus, the might and miracles of God are frequently seen there (Chao, 1988:106).

In other words, the central focus of their Christian life, what they call living the life of Christ, is to be found in their life of prayer, which expresses their ongoing dependence on God.

We noticed that among the Akamba that challenges of illness or hunger forced them to address issues of power. Religion, at least initially, is a matter of managing the powers that are believed to influence life in this world. We saw, moreover, that the power of God through Christ has come to replace all other avenues of power and has become the central focus of the believers' faith and devotion. Christ, in Kwame Bediako's words, has come to sit on the seat of the ancestors (1983).

What will those in a North American setting make of this? It cannot simply be applied to our totally different situation. But it is all immensely instructive. We noted, for example, in our case study from North America how devotional practices are undeveloped. The emphasis on making faith practical did not foster "empty" time with God. Here we need to learn, in the midst of our emotional loneliness, the relation between reconciliation and spirituality in the way the Mam have come to see it. We need to recover the centrality of dependence on God, which our sisters and brothers in China show us. Perhaps the Akamba case is the most helpful, for there we see the way a functional emphasis, so congenial to our American thinking, can lead to a life of prayer and dependence on Christ.

However, we must not leave the impression that the American church has nothing to offer in this conversation. The very preoccupation of American Christians with their development and emotional health points to the contribution they might make to a theology of the person. For, partly under Christian influence, we have come to understand a great deal about personal empowerment and individual liberty. Indeed, these ideas are now having a growing impact on newly liberated people in many parts of the world, where the nature and practice of democracy are being hotly debated. Any coherent understanding of spirituality must include the way in which the Gospel liberates people to recognize and develop their giftedness under God. While these things are sometimes emphasized in a narcissistic way in our setting, they are nevertheless important, and they must play a role in our inter-cultural conversation about spirituality.

When all is said and done, we must be able to learn from each other because when we finally stand before God, we will have brought with us all the glory and honor of the nations (Rev. 21:26). Meanwhile, we need each other. We all walk by faith and see through a glass darkly, for we are all standing at the place where our practice meets the presence of God; where the saints of all ages have struggled to see the way.

WORKS CITED

Kwame Bediako.
    1983.   "Biblical Christologies in the Context of African Tradi-
                tional Religions." In *Sharing Jesus in the Two Thirds
                World*. Edited by Vinay Samuel and Christ Sugden.
                Grand Rapids: Eerdmans.

Patricia Benner.
    1991.   "The Role of Experience, Narrative, and Community in
                Skilled Ethical Comportment." *Advances in Nursing
                Science*. 14/2.

Rudolph Bultmann.
    1960.   "Is Exegesis Without Presupposition Possible?" In
                Existence and Faith. Edited by S. M. Ogden. New York:
                Meridian.

Jonathan Chao, ed.
    1988.   *Wise and Serpents, Harmless as Doves: Christians in
                China Tell Their Story*. Pasadena: William Carey.

Clifford Geertz.
    1983.   *Local Knowledge: Further Essays in Interpretive An-
                thropology*. New York: Basic.

Roger Lundin, Anthony L. Thiselton, and Clarence Walhout.
    1985.   *The Responsibility of Hermeneutics*. Grand Rapids:
                Eerdmans.

Richard Mouw.
    1990.   *The God Who Commands*. South Bend: University of
                Notre Dame.

Richard A. Muller.
    1991.   *The Study of Theology: From Biblical Interpretation to
                Contemporary Formulation*. Grand Rapids: Zondervan.

Lesslie Newbigin.
    1989.   *The Gospel in a Pluralist Society*. Grand Rapids:
                Eerdmans.

William C. Placher.
    1989.   *Unapologetic Theology: A Christian Voice in Pluralis-
                tic Conversation*. Louisville: Westminster/John Knox.

David Scotchmer.
    1989.   "Symbols of Salvation: A Local Mayan Protestant
                Theology." *Missiology*. 17/3.

APPENDIX A

Traveling Preacher in North China

AN INTERVIEW WITH AN ITINERANT PREACHER IN CENTRAL CHINA IN THE SUMMER OF 1982

[Source: Interview 5.13 in *Wise as Serpents, Harmless as Doves*, by Jonathan Chao and Richard van Houten, 201–11]

From a very early age, I was willing to serve the Lord, and I preached the gospel to young children. Soon I was traveling all over—from Henan to Hubei, from Hubei to Shaanxi, from Shaanxi back to Hubei. In the 1960s I sometimes felt such a clear calling that wherever the Lord put me I would just talk about Him. So I knew clearly that the Lord wanted to use me and train me, and hence I was willing to give my whole life as a sacrifice to work for Him.

Since 1967 I have been amidst Christian brothers and sisters. At that time, Jiang Qing [Mao's wife] said that Christianity in China had already been put into a museum and that there were no more believers. But we brothers and sisters knew there were those who continued to preach from place to place. Thank the Lord that He has led His people through ten years of turmoil. The Lord has blessed us, telling us that, as we do this work of revival, Christ is with us.

Whenever the Church suffers great persecution, I remember what an old believer once prayed: "Oh Lord, we ask that You be with us in Your sacred work of revival. Thank you Lord." Once I heard that prayer I never forgot it. For ten years now, every time I pray I say, "Oh, Lord." This is truly the Lord's grace and mercy. Although I give

170

very little, the Lord receives my service. The Lord continues to train and lead me in the revival work as He puts me among believers all over the land. Thank the Lord for His mercy.

Just now I thought of more words the Lord had given us. The Lord does not give us worry-filled hearts, but hearts filled with peace and consolation. The Lord loves us, so what can people do to us? He whom we trust gives us strength so that we can do all this. Thank the Lord for His grace. We know we must obey our Lord, not men, because He gives us His precious power and faith. When we go preaching from village to village He gives us these words to console us. We know that those who trust in Him will be richly blessed.

We praise and thank the Lord that now the powerful fire of His revival is spreading. The miracles of His power extend to all the lands. The faith in the hearts of the itinerant preachers brings that fire to all places, and then the fire spreads from one place to the next, from one province to another. We can see that itinerant preachers are being used by God to do this kind of work. They are truly the treasure of the brothers and sisters as they do this revival work. They sacrifice everything as they set up underground churches and meetings and call on the brothers and sisters to serve the Lord.

FACING ARREST

Several times over the years I have come close to being arrested. Once, at a meeting in 1976 with a few hundred Christians, the police came in and ordered that everyone be arrested. We were right in the middle of prayer, and I was with the brothers and sisters praying in the courtyard. One of the sisters pulled me down and hid me. I wasn't sure what was going on since we were praying. Another covered me, and they took me to another place.

Once a Christian sister told me that in the event of a crisis during a meeting she knew of a small building where we could hide. If there was any danger, we could very quickly get to this place, and we surely wouldn't be discovered. We could eat there and hide out for a long time.

In another case, in 1977, when we were holding our meetings, a Party secretary who was drunk came and wanted to vent his anger. The brothers and sisters surrounded the itinerant preachers and surrounded the Party secretary too. The brothers and sisters had precisely coordinated it; they had bikes that seemed like wings as we fled. Some of the preachers were sent to the mountains to find a place to hide. Some of us were even sent to the Party secretary's house. As it turned out, his wife was a believer, along with his daughter and son. They had me stay with the son, and she told her son not to open the door when his father returned. Well, the Party secretary returned, but he didn't ask at all about me. That evening the brothers and sisters came to retrieve me and hide me elsewhere.

REVIVAL BEGINS, 1973–1980

Looking at my experience from the viewpoint of the Church's revival, I remember that on the eve of the revival we had asked ourselves just who it was that we believed in. To whom was the arm of Jehovah opening a clear path? We just believed in the power of God to protect our lives. We believed that His work was to be done. I decided to proceed with faith and confidence, and the Lord gave me that faith. At that time there were no churches set up. So we left for Hubei and preached wherever we went. We had the opportunity to share with those brothers and sisters, but they were very poor and I was saddened. But the Lord gave me strength and words. God consoled me and we suffered together. Oh, our Lord is a living Lord.

Although we are often cold toward God and refuse him, our God still is a loving God. The Lord gives us strength to meet with and share with the brothers and sisters. He leads our lives wherever we travel. Although this work is very tiring and our burden is heavy, at the beginning I felt compelled to give my feet to God. Once we started, it became a year's service, then two, then three. That was back in 1974; praise and thank the Lord for His mercy.

Back in 1973 we saw how the Lord was to carry out His own work in many different places. The Lord used miracles and the Spirit to bring the fire of revival to all these places. As a result, our scope of activities expanded and more came to believe. Everybody was extremely enthusiastic. Wherever we went we were not turned away. We were truly moved as we felt their great love for us. Sometimes they wouldn't let us go. We would go there and preach, and everyone would cry. We never decided ourselves where we wanted to go. We just listened to their demands about which area needed revival next, and we would go there.

The brothers and sisters were really hungry and thirsty for the Word in those days, and it seemed that nobody could get enough. I said in my heart, "Lord, I know too little about the Bible. I feel like a sheep that has to nurse all these little lambs. My milk has already been exhausted, and they are still sucking on my nipples." I really felt helpless. There were hundreds of brothers and sisters in the meeting, and I felt absolutely empty inside. So I stood up and cried. I said, "Lord. Look at all these people. They came for You, and nothing else can satisfy them. You put me in this place, but I really can do nothing. Lord, You have pity on them, and have pity on me." Every time I stood up and cried in my prayer like this, the Lord supplied me with His message out of His compassion for the brothers and sisters.

During this period, the feet of those that preached the good tidings were a true blessing. Wherever we went, dozens of people would follow behind us and form a big crowd. It was really a moving sight. We used to sing as we marched on the mountain path, whether it was day or night. Wherever we came to a family, the host would do his utmost to entertain us. They felt honored to be worthy to receive a servant of God. Sometimes those families that did not get this honor felt hurt. They thought they were unworthy. Sometimes they even envied those that got to entertain the preachers. Satan attacked many Christians by this means.

THE RETURN OF TSPM, 1980–PRESENT

The third period is one in which the cross of Calvary was transformed into an ornament for the daughters of Moab amidst persecutions and the roaring of the lion. Christianity was made into an ornament to adorn the harlot. For the sake of politics and diplomacy, Christianity was made a kind of showcase religion. Those Christians who had hidden themselves became enthusiastic once more. Actually, these people do love the Lord. But out of fear they confine their love for the Lord and their dedication to His work within the context of legality. If you told them it is illegal, then they would not come out. But Paul tells us that we must preach the gospel "in season and out of season." No matter the circumstances, we must sow the seed of the gospel.

There are also people who had been "church members" before but who had never really been saved. When the churches were reopened, they came back, arguing that they were the doorkeepers for the church. Why did they want to be doorkeepers for the church? They wanted to obtain legal recognition from the government so that they could transfer their residences to the city or obtain some specific position. They were willing to be ornaments in order that their conditions might be improved. These people entered the Church with ulterior motives and caused a lot of confusion. From a state of purity and devotion, she was led into a condition where she just wandered aimlessly without knowing where to go. Under these circumstances, what kind of a harlot church have we become? How can the Lord lead the Chinese Church to revival in this kind of situation?

We are still in the third period, although it might seem to have lasted for a long time. But we need to go deeper into this matter. During our co-workers' meeting, we saw three ways in which we can deal with this quasi-church: (1) We may act like Phinehas, who pierced through the harlot with his spear; (2) we may blow our horns and trumpets to warn people to come out from the evil place, as in the book of Joshua; and (3) we may grind these people—like the golden calf—to pieces by the truth of the Bible. But the present period will continue for a while.

DAILY LIFE OF AN ITINERANT PREACHER

I didn't have time to look back before, but this year the Lord often wanted me to look back. Before the Chinese New Year, the believers at Fangmaoshan had three days of special meetings. They had been having frequent contacts with us in the fellowship of the Bible, and we felt we had a share in their salvation as well as in the building of their church. But I had not been there for a long time. One reason for this is that I have to spend a lot of time in Bible ministry, and at the same time I have to take care of my regular work. Another reason is that my mother was very sick during that time. Under their persistent requests, however, three of us brothers went to Fangmaoshan just before New Year's day. We held three days of meetings there. Each night the meeting lasted almost till daybreak. It rained and snowed on the last night. After the meeting broke up, the brothers and sisters took us to the railway station on their bicycles.

The next morning at about 4 a.m. we arrived in Tacheng. A brother who works at the Tacheng bus station took us to a sister's home with the bus he drove. After a short rest there, we caught another bus home in a heavy rain. (A brother was almost frozen.) When we got home the family had already gone to bed.

The next day was New Year's day, and we fellowshipped with brothers and sisters at home. On the second day of the new year, we went to another place to have fellowship with brothers and sisters there, which was followed by a baptismal service. Several brothers and sisters were baptized. On the third day after New Year's day I went home, and with my two sisters I went to visit my aunt, who was seventy-five years old. She had been a believer for forty to fifty years, and lately she had been expecting each day that the Lord would come and take her to heaven. On the following day, an annual co-workers' conference started at Tacheng. On the first day we fasted and prayed. Messages were given on each of the following three days. The main theme of these messages was the harlot church, and the believers were exhorted to deal with her as Phinehas dealt with the Midianite woman.

On the ninth day, we arrived at Funing in Xinsui, where a co-workers' conference was starting. The conference was conducted in a fellowship and Bible study style. The theme of the conference was the training of preachers and the propagation of the gospel. The emphasis was letting the young people testify of how they magnify the power of the Holy Spirit in their life outside the church and in their preaching of the gospel, and of how they feel the presence of God as they do this. Thank God, all the conferees saw the solemn responsibility that we have to preach the gospel and realized that He that is with us is much greater than he that is with them. They come to attack us with knives and spears and brazen shields, but we attack them with the name of the Lord of hosts. The atmosphere of the meeting climbed to a high pitch on this, and everybody's spirit got a lift.

On the tenth, my sister arrived from home. She said my aunt prayed every day, saying, "Oh Lord, please send my nephew back, for I am about to depart from this world." She had not eaten for three days. There was neither fever nor cold, and she was not suffering from any particular illness or pain. My sister wanted me to go home right away, saying my seventy-five year old aunt could die at any moment. My aunt prayed daily, "Lord, why are You keeping me in the world now that I can no longer preach or serve You? I am not anxious to go home and enjoy myself, but since I am no longer useful in the world, You may just as well take me to heaven." Her son was a cadre in the brigade and had not believed in the Lord. As they talked with her, she expressed her wish that she wanted to have a Christian funeral service after she died and that she wanted me to go back and lead the service. I had a feeling that I ought to go back.

I arrived home on the twelfth, and my aunt died on the morning of the fifteenth. The funeral service was held on the eighteenth and was attended by more than a thousand believers. In the service, we also preached from the Bible on topics like the origin of man, the redemption of Christ, and the resurrection. A brother brought an amplifier and a tape recorder. So the whole proceeding was taped and broadcast. Since the service was held by the graveside in an open field, a great number of people could hear the message, including a lot of non-believers.

BIBLE STUDIES ORGANIZED

On the eighteenth we arrived at Feng Song's place. As we fellowshipped with each other that evening, a sister named Guo with tears in her eyes implored us to go to her place. We were thinking of establishing a Bible study group in the border region in those days, and we thought this might be the leading of the Lord. So, together with Feng Song, fifteen of us started the next day for Lingbo Commune. At Annan we established the first Bible study group, which met every Monday.

Perhaps I can explain here how we set up these Bible study groups. For those young converts who were desirous of knowing more about the Bible, we organized Bible study sessions on each night of the week in different places. These sessions lasted for two or more hours each. We first trained some brothers and sisters, then sent them out two by two [two brothers or two sisters] to visit the Bible study groups, each on a different night of the week according to a prearranged schedule. It took them a week to complete the circuit.

In our Bible studies, we follow two principles: (1) learn basic doctrines of the Bible; and(2) provide messages that are most needed in this generation. As for visiting pastors or evangelists, they are free to preach on any topic according to the moving of the Holy Spirit. In other words, we don't want to formalize or generalize the topics of the messages. In this way our brothers and sisters are always supplied with fresh and vital messages that are most suited to the current climate. After the two brothers or sisters have released all the messages that they are burdened with, they will be led to another cycle, and two brothers or sisters from that cycle will take over the first cycle. In this way, the brothers and sisters in all the cycles will always have fresh and different messages to hear.

As they teach others, they themselves are being trained. After they have been teaching for three or five weeks or, in some cases, seven to eight weeks, they will have a recess. During the recess they will be divided into groups and assigned different Bible portions to study. Through this they gain experience not only in preaching but also in leading Bible study sessions and other meetings.

After we agreed on the basic teaching materials, we printed several hundred copies of basic Bible doctrines. Now we plan to print the "Study of the Truth," "How to Study the Bible," and "Exercise of the Truth," and to send copies of each of these to each Bible study group.

MINISTERING ON ROAD

On the twentieth, we arrived at Palingmiao. There was a brother named Wan who was quite a warrior for the truth. He was a writer before he accepted Christ. After he was saved, he didn't have any spiritual exercise and received no discipline from the Church. Out of his own zeal he went to Ningbo to get Bibles. But he didn't get any Bibles. His money was taken away, he was arrested and locked up, and he almost lost his life. Finally, he and his wife begged their way back, but the church's money was all gone. His spirit got a severe blow from this, and he was quite depressed for a long time. Later he got in touch with Brother Feng Song and was warmed up again after some fellowship with him. Now he is the pastor of that village. According to their need and our guidance from the Lord, we hurried to that village, where we had fellowship with the brothers and sisters and established a Bible study group.

On the twenty-first we got to Wangping where we established a Bible study group. On the twenty-second we returned to Annan, where we established another Bible study point. Brother Feng Song went to another place to preach the salvation of the cross. I felt very tired since I had to preach every day before Brother Feng came. After he came, he took over the evening meeting, and the Lord really worked. I was so tired that I went to bed shortly after nine. Then I heard a sister crying aloud downstairs. So I got up and went downstairs and sat with her during her confession. It turned out that she had committed adultery since she was eight. Then she seduced her husband to commit adultery with her own sister. Her own daughter also committed adultery in order to get a job. Some of the sins she committed were really queer. But the Holy Spirit got hold of her, and she confessed her sins until seven o'clock the next morning. None of us got any sleep the whole night. As she finished her confession and was realized from her bondage, she lay on the floor as if totally paralyzed, like a newborn baby.

On the twenty-fourth, like we were having our meeting in the afternoon, Lai Deliu and Peng Shengong came on their bicycles. After the evening meeting we hurried to Wendeng at two o'clock in the morning. There were about 700 brothers and sisters there. Then we continued to Wuting and entered a brother's home at about four o'clock. Since we had been without sleep for several days and nights, we all felt very tired. At the insistence of the brothers and sisters there, we decided to stay and have some sleep.

As we woke up later in the morning, we had already gathered a group of people for the meeting, and we had to preach again. I talked first, followed by Brother Feng. As he talked, I quietly slipped away. On the way I met an old lady who was coming for the meeting. So I asked her to tell the brothers there that I had gone ahead and asked them to follow on as soon as the meeting was over. Together we hurried to Tonglan, about ten miles away, where another meeting was under way. There was a young couple there that had a problem. The young woman insisted on staying with one of the men. Without approval from the church or consultation with other brothers and sisters, they began living together and exerting a bad influence on others. But they were still very fervent in serving the Lord. When we arrived the meeting started right away. We dealt specifically with this problem in our preaching according to the truth of the Bible. After some private conversations with the brothers and sisters following the meeting, we told the young couple to talk with their parents and get their understanding and permission [to marry].

On the twenty-sixth we returned to Lingbo. The believers there tried to get us to stay with them, but we insisted on moving forward. As a result of this conflict, we missed two trains, and we decided to walk twenty miles in the night. On the way, we met an itinerant preacher from Mingtang. He was a blacksmith by profession, but he also preached the gospel and led many people to the Lord. He had just returned from the mountain district when we met, and he told us that they were going to pray for a sick sister that evening. That sister also loved the Lord, but once she had thrown the Bible to the floor, and Satan had entered her heart. She got sick and was in shock, so she was sent to the hospital. There was a faint beating of her heart, but she had been lying there motionless for four or five days. Everybody prayed for her. Satan also attacked her mother. Under these circumstances the believers were so frightened that they ceased to pray, thinking that Satan was too powerful. We told him that we were coming exactly for this purpose. So we hastened to that place together and prayed for the sister. It was very cold and somebody started a fire. The doctor said the patient was going to die. According to the custom in Henan, an unmarried daughter was not allowed to die in the house. So they built a booth in the yard and put her there to die. We all knelt down and prayed with tears that the Lord would raise her up from the dead. The Lord had risen from the dead, and He also raised Lazarus from the dead. Likewise He could also raise up our sister. But, on the other hand, we prayed that not our will but the will of the Holy Spirit be done. After we prayed we hurried to Wuting the same night. Later we heard that the sister had died. The view of many on this was that when she threw the Bible to the floor she uttered many blasphemous words—that the whole incident was a warning from the Lord to the Church.

So that is my schedule. I am not alone in this situation. All the brothers and sisters who do itinerant evangelism are in the same boat. You see, we have quite a large area to cover, and it will take us a terribly long time to make rounds if we don't squeeze our schedule. We feel that we have a lot of things to say to the brothers and sisters, especially to those whom we don't get to visit very often. They love to have us preach to them, and this overrides their concern for our bodies. We, too, are encouraged by their love, and with the support of the Holy Spirit we generally don't feel tired when we minister to them. Praise God for His grace.

APPENDIX B

Protestant Maya Text
(abridged)

(MAM CHRISTIAN)

[Source: Narrative by Félix López, Mam Protestant; collected and translated by David G. Scotchmer]

My name is Félix López. I have lived in a small cantón called River Rock in the town of Three Drums. I was a very poor one and there (at home) I worked constantly in the fields.

In the past I would go to the coast and once for 4 straight years. For 15 months I [walked] labored in the cotton fields and for 4 more months in the coffee fields.

We suffered very much as we worked [walked] in the heat. But that was not all, for I also became very, very ill, for in the coast there exists many illnesses. I used to be in Catholic Action.

In the church with the priest is where I celebrated first communion. For three years I remained in this church and I was a teacher of the people and I taught the doctrines to the people so they could memorize it.

But I did not understand what was my own faith, because there was not a very good explanation in Catholic Action, and never was the Word of God taught (showed) to us, that is, that which is in the Bible.

There came a day when I believed. It was one day when I heard

God's word. I was very happy and I was even amazed, for then I recognized [knew] about the lord [owner], Jesus Christ.

I then received him as my one savior, and as my lord [owner] forever, and as my one guardian for my life. Clearly, I felt God's favor from the word of God and from the hymns when I heard them.

I then made an effort to read the word of Our Father God in the Bible, and I became a helper in my congregation because in this congregation there was not one who was older and a believer.

We waited and worked with a brother; Juan was his name. I became a beginning preacher. Only that which I understood was what I explained to my brethren, the same as it says in the Bible. Nine years have gone by since I believed [and as a member] in the Protestant Church of San Juan.

This is the church where I believed and where I have been happiest and where I began to be of some small usefulness. I have worked a bit in God's work. And then I began in a literary program [so that people could learn to read, that is, those who do not know how to read]. It was in this program that we began to work and we were very happy, because it was my desire to help even a little bit among each of our older brothers.

Further, I was part of the youth society. There was such a group for youth in the church, and I was active as a committee member. So we worked, in that we went to many distant worship services.

It was when I had barely started to work in the literary program, that is, teaching reading to people who do not know how to read, when those who take away (grab) young men, those known as commissioners sent by the army (that is, the ones assigned to gather together the people so that they may be carried to the military headquarters), then on this very day, I had not heard that those who catch (were there), but nevertheless there arrived some 20 or so in all and I was carried off in the town of San Juan. They put me in jail; then we were put into a truck, an enormous one that carried us, those who were caught and taken to the military base.

Then I became extremely sad because in that moment when we were carried off there was no way for me to get out. I had been continuously sick in these days. When I arrived in Xela, I thought they might free me because of the illness in my body.

But when I told the leader of the soldiers, those who watched the people, they did not believe me; they said "You are fine (you are OK). You will be very useful," they said. When we then went into the examination by the doctor of the base, all the ones who were sick were separated apart.

I was then waiting to be separated out from them. When the doctor came to me, he told me that I was just fine. He did not find my illness in my body. Then we were taken all the way to Jutiapa to be in a class or in the training to learn how to do those things that are done by the military. The training there was for three months in order for us to finish. When we went we were all so sad, everyone together who were with me.

When we arrived there, that's when I became really sad. First, because of the word that went out to those of my house, my father, and my older brother and my younger brothers. Also because there was no time to talk with my older brothers and younger brothers in the church, those of the youth society, and also because of the literary work with those brothers with whom we worked together, which was a great joy for us to be in this work together.

There were those who remembered me (went to check on me), but it was impossible as we had gone far away. I was so very sad because of this. But I did something (acted) in a certain way.

I pretended that apparently I was not sad, and acted as if I were really happy. I showed myself before my commander as if I did not have any fear in me. Then because they observed my manner, they marveled because of it and were pleased, and said "This man here is not afraid and he is very smart, too," they said. During the whole training and the teaching I showed this attitude to the corporal and the sergeant.

I was then very careful about it, but most of all I trusted in God. My faith was in the Lord Jesus Christ. He is the one I trusted in as my helper and my strength every day.

Even though I suffered a lot, (but) Christ was with me. Then it was due to God's favor (grace) that he helped me. When we were lined up listening to the class they gave us, and I gave my attention to it, I could do these things even though the tough things but God helped me because I was trusting in him; and I quickly learned when they showed us something. (Because) when I arrived there, the corporal and the sergeant, they all of them with their authority, are very tough (strong) and fearsome. For example, if they came to look us over, we were not to move an inch once we were all ordered in line.

If anyone was looking in another direction, immediately he was hit by the leader. It did occur to me to flee when I saw how tough it got; I said, "I'll never survive this." But the commanders were always guarding day and night, and we were not allowed out for free time except to leave briefly once in a while. Because of all this I trusted even more in God. And I would think, "What am I going to do, since I can't really speak in Spanish? And I really don't understand their talk because they only speak in Spanish." When I look [back] carefully, I really couldn't talk in Spanish.

When I arrived among them, then I began little by little to understand this talk and how it went and what I was to understand, and it helped a lot as I learned to talk more in Spanish. Little by little my fear and shame subsided, and I trusted even more in God. There was also a good rapport among us with the people or with the corporal who told me, "You have a good attitude because you pay attention," he said. They talked well with me.

When they gave us something to do together with everyone, we were not able to do it well, then we all suffered severly. No matter if it was the fault of only one person all of us were punished because of it.

In one of these moments when we were suffering, I thought, "I can't make it," because if we can't do it all, we will be punished plenty. We suffered plenty and we were trained plenty.

But in a way, even though we suffered considerably, all the more the fear left me, and I was determined even more to do it so that we all would not be punished, and I was able to do things even a little better because of the fear of not doing the best we could. There were two times when we nearly all died due to the suffering they gave us, because they had no mercy for us, and there were no favors they would show, not the least.

In this period I felt so bad and my illness kept getting worse and worse. But because I could do a little, one day they put me on the guard duty at the barracks, and when I was left I did not go with the rest. I stayed behind to guard and I was to stay alone and guard by myself, so that I would not mess it up. The others, if they stayed to guard the room, would always suffer lots and they would be punished because at times they would say one thing to them and it would not be done. And at other times they would become afraid of the rest, and would not tell them what they had to do a job for them, like to sweep. When I was left in charge, I hustled to do everything, even the little that I did understand.

And I gave work to the rest to do, whether to sweep or wash in the house, or to go and polish their boots. And occasionally if, for example, the commanders wanted to get everyone together quickly I would go and tell everyone.

For this I was not punished and thus did not suffer lots when I was left to guard the room. Little by little they trusted me and little by little my fear subsided, for as I did my work they did not speak to me. And they trusted me (the leaders) and they were happy with me. Then after our three months training, they took us to a more distant place, all the way up to the Petén. When I arrived there I was really in pain and my illness was really severe and it became critical and I only waited for God's favor in order to see what he would do. Then the training became even more severe, the commanders were harder and tougher on us, and I told them, "I can't go on. If only you would give me some medicine, because I have been sick since I was taken into the army." The commanders did not believe me. They summoned the medicine, but they did not give me any. For in their eyes I was lying, and the training became even harder.

Even as we learned to do a little more, they would give us harder things to do. This training would not have been too bad for a healthy person, but due to the illness I only felt like I was going to die.

I asked the commander if maybe I could have a moment off but there was no way and they did not believe me. (Because) the manner of these people (those in the army) is not like we treat others at home.

Those of us at home maybe we yell or we do as we please, and we may get angry, but there it was not the same. Even if you were sick, they do not believe you. Until they see that you have fallen or until you cannot walk, then they believe you and take you to get medicine or kick you out. For me at this particular time.

I was more in prayer and in trusting God than ever asking, "What am I to do and what will happen to me?" I was not thinking that I might get out or not. I was only waiting on God's favor. But God answered my prayer and although I had not left, the thought came to me that it would be better for me to go home, and so I left. So when I left I walked along the road, seeing different people on my journey, some who were workers or were officials in the army, but they said nothing to me.

Later I arrived and I arrived home very happy. Nothing happened on the journey and I was not stopped by them. When I arrived I was truly amazed and I thought about it. In truth, God is all powerful because he helped me on my journey.

"I have been watched over and taken care of," I said in my prayer to God, but I was so afraid when I first arrived because there might be an order given to capture me. But nothing happened and I was not seized neither by the military commissioner nor by anyone else. Perhaps in this too God was helping. And Our Father God has a special desire and I serve him. For when I returned I began to read again the word of Our Father God and I began to teach myself in the word.

There are several points that I find very wonderful. Things that I saw in the army, and now I understand, when I went to read them in the word of Our Father God. Some of them were very helpful to me.

All of this has served me as a school to understand more clearly just how to follow Jesus Christ, how to be a soldier of Christ. How to put these things into my life in order to tell you how I walked, how I succeeded or failed, and how when I wondered about the church or the brethren and asked are we doing what Our Lord said or are we not?

On this score I have come to learn a bit about the world of Our Father God. I have really felt the favor of Our Father God. And God truly has chosen me to become his servant, to go and preach his word to do as he wants.

Although there is not a lot I can do but what God has given me will be used by me for him. I have become a worker in the church during the last two years, preaching God's word and teaching to our older and younger brothers who do not yet understand the word well. Because of this I have come to know in truth that God has a plan for me because he helped me get out of the army and then brought me back to a ministry. And in this work there is no one who elevates himself to do the work of God.

I have been gladdened by one verse found in Timothy that says: "It is God that has given understanding to his servants in order that they do the work of God."

The mind (wisdom) of God gives us is a knowledge of very great authority, in order that we might be able to provide an explanation that is clearer for our brothers as well as an explanation that is softer (easier to understand) in order that they might know more about the faith in Our Lord. With this in mind and for this very reason, I am working in the church. I am active somewhat among the brethren and the brethren held an election or rather picked a worker.

They chose me to work in a program for the production of literature in Spanish, in order that I work with literature production as well as sell books, like the New Testament or other similar material with God's word in it, and also the production of some literature in Mam.

In the army or where there is any kind of order and some kind of law, if one is told now it is imperative to do something, it is not to be forgotten, and there is no room to say "I can't do it," supposedly by someone. That which has been said must be done even if it is tough but it is essential to be done. That is the way man's laws are.

That is the law of man on earth, if you are not accountable to Our Father God. Jesus Christ is the one leader for us, a captain, a general, one who gives wise counsel. He has more authority than that of the people.

We essentially are fearful of people with much authority. But Our Father Jesus Christ has greater power, and much more authority than do these people. That's because God's law is a very holy authority, and more than anything it speaks strongly about our hearts.

It speaks about our lives and how they need to be opened, about how we may become stronger believers, who are upright and true in our faith, like a soldier of Jesus Christ.

What is it that God observes in our behavior? How does Our Father Jesus Christ look on us? Are we doing what we do with joy? Do we go quickly and do what God has told us to do? Do we do it just to get by or do we just not want to go and do what we must?

Now then Our Father Jesus Christ will probably not come here and hit you. But he is observing to see if you are an honest to goodness soldier of Jesus Christ, to see if you go and do the work of God, that which he wants done or are you just barely getting by.

When we enter into worship, this moment should be used eagerly to hear the word of Our Father God and we should think about it eagerly. When worship is over we should have a clear idea and hopefully a bit of advice for ourselves. Because this moment is a time for us to nourish ourselves spiritually. But not just this; rather we are to put into use what we have heard and do it eagerly.

If we do not give ourselves to eating the spiritual food, and if all we do is look at it when food is prepared on the table, but do not eat from it, the food will remain only as food and will not be of benefit when Our Lord Jesus Christ comes. What will you say to him? "I'm just now on my way to eat," you say.

It is essential that you eat first, it is imperative to eat your food before you have to be told by him, "Now you will leave the table." Because when he comes to say this word even though you are hungry and even if you are trusting you will not have a drop to drink or to eat as there's no more time. The time will be over for us.

This is the story of my life that has transpired. It really is not much but these things I have seen. These are the things I have done and I have experienced and are what I have told here.

BIBLIOGRAPHY

Abesamis, Carlos H. "A Third Look at Jesus: A Catechetical Guidebook for Bible Facilitators." Quezon City, Philippines: Claretian, 1988.

Adeney, David H. *China: Church's Long March.* Ventura: Regal; Singapore: OMF, 1985.

Amin, Mohammed, and Peter Moll. *Portraits of Africa.* London: Harvill Press, 1983.

Annis, Sheldon. *God and Production in a Guatemalan Town.* Austin: University of Texas, 1987.

Auerbach, Erich. *Mimesis: The Representation of Reality in Western Literature.* Princeton: Princeton University, 1953.

Balmer, Randall. *Mine Eyes Have Seen the Glory: A Journey Into the Evangelical Subculture in America.* Oxford: Oxford University, 1989.

Banks, Robert. *All the Business of Life: Bringing Theology Down to Earth.* Sutherland, NSW, Australia: Albatross, 1987.

Barna, George. *The Frog in the Kettle.* Ventura: Regal, 1990.

Baum, Gregory. *Religion and Alienation: A Theological Reading of Sociology.* New York: Paulist, 1975.

Bediako, Kwame. "Biblical Christologies in the Context of African Traditional Religions." In *Sharing Jesus in the Two Thirds World.* Ed. Vinay Samuel and Christ Sugden. Grand Rapids: Eerdmans, 1983.

Bellah, Robert, Richard Masden, William M. Sullivan, Ann Swidler, and Steven M. Tipton. *Habits of the Heart: Individualism and Commitment in American Life.* Berkeley: University of California, 1985.

Beltran, Benigno P. *The Christology of the Inarticulate: An Inquiry into the Filipino Understanding of Jesus the Christ.* Manila: Divine Word, 1987.

Benner, Patricia. "The Role of Experience, Narrative, and Community in Skilled Ethical Comportment." *Advances in Nursing Science.* 14/2 (1991).

Berger, Peter, and Thomas Luckmann. *The Social Construction of Reality: A Treatise in the Sociology of Knowledge.* Garden City: Doubleday, 1967.

Berger, Peter, Brigitte Berger, and Hansfried Kellner. *The Homeless Mind: Modernization and Consciousness.* Hammondsworth: Penguin, 1984.

Berger, Peter. *The Sacred Canopy: Elements of a Sociological Theory of Religion.* Garden City: Doubleday, 1969.

Bossy, John. *Christianity in the West: 1400–1700.* Oxford: Oxford University, 1985.

Bricker, Victoria Reifler. *The Indian Christ, The Indian King: The Historical Substrate of Maya Myth and Ritual.* Austin: University of Texas, 1981.

Bulatao, Jaime. "Hiya." *Philippine Studies.* (1964): 12.

Bultmann, Rudolph. "Is Exegesis Without Presupposition Possible?" In *Existence and Faith.* Ed. S. M. Ogden. New York: Meridian, 1960.

Butler, Jon. *Awash in a Sea of Faith: Christianizing the American People.* Cambridge, Mass.: Harvard University, 1989.

Campbell, Will D. "Nit-Picking on a Fine Book." *Christianity and Crisis.* 44/2 (Feb. 20, 1984): 42–43.

Chang, Ming-Che. *Jump Over Mountain Mists and Rapids; The Struggle of My Believing.* Seattle: OMF, n.d.

Chao, Jonathan. *Wise as Serpents, Harmless as Doves: Christians in China Tell Their Story.* Ed. Richard Van Houten. Pasadena: William Carey; Hong Kong: Chinese Church Research Center, 1988.

Cooke, Bernard. *The Distancing of God.* Minneapolis: Augsburg Fortress, 1990.

Dyrness, William. "A Unique Opportunity: Christianity in the World Today, a Globe Encircling Appraisal." In *MARC 14th Mission Handbook.* Monrovia: Missions Advanced Research and Communication Center; Grand Rapids: Zondervan, 1989.

_____. *How Does America Hear the Gospel.* Grand Rapids: Eerdmans, 1989.

————. *Learning About Theology from the Third World.* Grand Rapids: Zondervan, 1990.

Earle, Duncan. "The Metaphor of the Day in Quiche: Notes on the Nature of Everyday Life." In *Symbol and Meaning Beyond the Closed Community: Essays in Mesoamerican Ideas.* Studies on Culture and Society, Vol. 1. Ed. Gary H. Gossen. Albany: State University of New York, 1986.

Elwood, Douglas J. "Christian Theology in an Asian Setting: The Gospel and Chinese Intellectual Culture." *Southeast Asia Journal of Theology.* 16/2 (1975): 1–16.

Enriquez, Virgilio G. *Indigenous Psychology and National Consciousness.* Tokyo: Institute for the Study of Languages and Cultures of Asia and Africa, 1989.

Espiritu, Socorro, Mary R. Hollnsteiner, Chesster L. Hunt, Luis Q. Lacar, and Lourdes R. Quisumbing. *Sociology in the New Philippine Setting.* Manila: Alemar, 1976.

Frank, Douglas W. *Less Than Conquerors: How Evangelicals Entered the Twentieth Century.* Grand Rapids: Eerdmans, 1986.

Gaede, Stanley D. *Where Gods May Dwell: On Understanding the Human Condition.* Grand Rapids: Zondervan, 1985.

Geertz, Clifford. *Interpretation of Cultures.* New York: Basic, 1973.

————. *Local Knowledge: Further Essays in Interpretive Culture.* New York: Basic, 1983.

Gehman, Richard J. *Ancestor Relations Among Three African Societies.* D.Miss. diss., Fuller Theological Seminary School of World Mission, 1985.

Hatch, Nathan. *The Democratization of American Christianity.* New Haven: Yale, 1989.

Hollnsteiner, Mary R., and Alfonso de Guzman II, eds. *Four Readings in Filipino Values.* Quezon City: Ateneo de Manila University, 1973.

Hollnsteiner, Mary R. "Urbanization of Metro Manila." In *Changing Southeast Asian Cities.* Eds. Y. M. Yeung and C. P. Lo. Oxford: Oxford University, 1976.

————. "Folk Catholicism in the Philippines." In *Society Culture and the Filipino.* Ed. Mary R. Hollnsteiner. Quezon City: Institute of Philippine Culture, 1979.

Holmer, Paul. *The Grammar of Faith.* San Francisco: Harper and Row, 1978.

Hunter, James Davison. *American Evangelicalism: The Coming Generation.* New Brunswick: Rutgers University, 1983.

Johnston, Robert K. "Acculturation or Inculturation? A Contemporary Evangelical Theology of the Atonement." *Covenant Quarterly* 46 (1988): 200–214.

Lader, James I."Getting Emotional About Quality." *The Quality Review,* (Summer 1988): 32–36.

Lundin, Roger, Anthony L. Thiselton, and Clarence Walhout. *The Responsibility of Hermeneutics.* Grand Rapids: Eerdmans, 1985.

Lynch, Frank, and Alfonso de Guzman II, eds. *Four Readings in Filipino Values.* Quezon City: Ateneo de Manila Univ. Press (Institute of Philippine Culture), 1973.

MacIntyre, Alasdair. *After Virtue.* 2d ed. South Bend: University of Notre Dame, 1984.

Maggay, Melba P. "The Indigenous Religious Consciousness: Some Implications for Mission." *Patmos.* 7/1 (1991).

Mbiti, John S. *African Religions and Philosophy.* London: Heinemann, 1969.

————. *New Testament Eschatology in an African Background.* Oxford: Oxford University, 1971.

————. *The Bible and Theology in African Christianity.* Nairobi: Oxford University, 1986.

Menchu, Rigoberta. *I, Rigoberta Menchu: An Indian Woman in Guatemala.* Ed. Elisabeth Burgos-Debray. London: Verso Editions, 1984.

Ming-dao, Wang. *A Stone Made Smooth.* Southampton: Mayflower, 1981.

Miranda-Feliciano, Evelyn. *Filipino Values and Our Christian Faith.* Manila: OMF, 1990.

Mouw, Richard. *The God Who Commands.* South Bend: Notre Dame University, 1990.

Muller, Richard A. *The Study of Theology: From Biblical Interpretation to Contemporary Formulation.* Grand Rapids: Zondervan, 1991.

Murphy, Nancey. *Theology in the Age of Scientific Reasoning.* Ithaca: Cornell University, 1990.

Newbigin, Lesslie. *The Gospel in a Pluralistic Society.* Grand Rapids: Eerdmans, 1989.

Noll, Mark, Nathan Hatch, and George Marsden. *The Search for Christian America.* Westchester, Ill: Crossway, 1983.

Placher, William C. *Unapologetic Theology: A Christian Voice in Pluralistic Conversation.* Louisville: Westminster/John Knox, 1989.

Schreiter, Robert. *Constructing Local Theologies.* Maryknoll: Orbis, 1985.

Scotchmer, David. "Convergence of the Gods: Comparing Traditional Maya and Christian Maya Cosmologies." In *Symbol and Meaning Beyond the Closed Community: Essays in Mesoamerican Ideas.* Ed. Gary H. Gossen. Albany: State University of New York, 1986.

————. Appended testimony of Mam believer is listed in text as PM (Protestant Maya), 1986.

————. "Life of the Heart: A Maya Protestant Spirituality." In *World Spirituality: An Encyclopedia.* Ed. Gary H. Gossen. Forthcoming.

————."Symbols of Salvation: A Local Mayan Protestant Theology." *Missiology.* 17/3 (July 1989): 293–310.

Sofola, 'Zulu. "The Theatre in the Search for African Authenticity." In *African Theology En Route.* Ed. Kifi Appiah-Jubi and Sergio Torres. Maryknoll: Orbis, 1979.

Stendahl, Krister. "The Apostle Paul and the Introspective Conscience of the West." In *Paul Among Jews and Gentiles.* Philadelphia: Fortress, 1976.

Taylor, Charles. *Sources of the Self: The Making of Modern Identity.* Cambridge, Mass.: Harvard University, 1990.

Taylor, John V. *The Primal Vision: Christian Presence and African Religions.* London: SCM, 1963.

Tedlock, Barbara. "A Phenomenological Approach to Religious Change in Highland Guatemala." In *Heritage of Conquest: Thirty Years Later.* Ed. Carl Kendall, John Hawkins, and Kaurel Bossen. Albuquerque: University of New Mexico, 1983.

Thiong'O, Ngugi Wa. *Decolonizing the Mind: The Politics of Language in African Literature*. Nairobi: Heinemann Kenya, 1986.

Unpublished testimonies (where unattributed in the text).

Van Allmen, Daniel. "The Birth of Theology." *International Review of Missions* 44 (1975): 37–55.

Wing-Hung, Lam. *Chinese Theology in Construction*. Pasadena: William Carey, 1983.

Wuthnow, Robert. *Acts of Compassion: Caring for Others and Helping Ourselves*. Princeton: Princeton University Press, 1991.

INDEX

Printed in the United States
1172600001B/235-294

9 780310 535812